The Future of Human Resources

The Future of Human Resources

Unlocking Human Potential

Tim Baker

BUSINESS EXPERT PRESS

Leader in applied, concise business books

First published in 2022 by
Business Expert Press, LLC
222 East 46th Street, New York, NY 10017
www.businessexpertpress.com

ISBN-13: 978-1-63742-229-8 (paperback)
ISBN-13: 978-1-63742-228-1 (e-book)

Business Expert Press Human Resource Management and
Organizational Behavior Collection

First edition: 2022

10 9 8 7 6 5 4 3 2 1

*To HR professionals wherever they may be, devoted
to their profession, and striving to create
employee-centered organizations.*

Description

The tired cliché that *employees are our greatest asset* is false. It's unlocking the *potential* of employees that's the greatest asset. COVID-19 has accelerated an examination of HR and all that it does. Releasing people's potential at work is key to business success more than ever.

The Future of Human Resources confronts the conventional employment practices of selecting, inducting, developing, rewarding, and exiting employees. This book is a comprehensive blueprint for HR professionals to make the necessary changes to accommodate a new mentality.

Thirteen traditional practices are challenged, and fresh, practical pathways offered. *The Future of Human Resources* sheds light on what works, what doesn't work, and why. It shines a spotlight on an uncertain pathway forward for the world of work.

By critiquing the employee's organizational journey—from starting to parting—the aim of the book is to cultivate the right environment for people at work to prosper in the postpandemic world.

Dr. Tim Baker, according to leadership guru, Marshall Goldsmith, is "one of today's most influential HR experts." He offers new insights about what's still considered conventional wisdom, such as employee inductions, job descriptions, and succession planning.

The central idea of *The Future of Human Resources* is the imperative for companies to adopt an employee-centered approach. Baker's employee lifecycle model tracks the familiar passage employees take in their employment route, from job interview to exit interview.

Keywords

human resources; trends in human resources; HR; managing performance; performance management; employee development; job design; employee engagement; attraction and retention

Contents

Testimonials

"Tim asks timely and pertinent questions and offers equally relevant suggestions. While scientific control methods may have been reliable and relevant in the last century, we live in a fast and mind-blowingly changing world. His well-researched and thoughtful book encourages us to evolve or ... become irrelevant. This is a 'must read' for HR practitioners and senior executives." —**Bill Lee-Emery, Keynote Speaker, Corporate facilitator and author of *How To Be Bulletproof From Criticism.***

"As we navigate the impact of the Covid pandemic, there has never been a more important nor opportune time to challenge and improve our ways of managing work. Tim's timely, thought-provoking book challenges some of the long-held mindsets and perspectives and offers an alternative path for the future of HR." —**David Concannon, Head of Insights & Strategy, Employer Branding Australia**

"Dr. Tim Baker has written an easy-to-read, comprehensive, and forward-thinking book on where HR needs to position itself for the future. There are some brilliant insights and a must read for those who are trying to get the very best from their employees." —**Dr. Peter W. Beven, Director QUTeX Open Professional Education, GSB, QUT**

"Reading The Future of Human Resources *will help you build, lead, and inspire teams to flourish in the post-Covid world. Tim Baker provides insights—based on the latest research, examples from real world business success, and his decades in leadership and organizational development—to help you transform the employee experience. It's a practical, hands-on approach that you can read now and apply tomorrow."* —**Clio Robertson, Senior L&D Specialist, Team Management Systems**

Acknowledgments

Thanks to Dr. Mike Provitera for his guidance, reassurance, and encouragement. I also acknowledge Scott Isenberg, managing executive editor of Business Express Press for showing faith in the ideas in this book and guiding me through the editorial process so professionally. The talented Charlene Kronstedt for creating great cover design for this book, with a minimum amount of fuss.

Introduction

Frederick Taylor conducted time and motion studies on the Ford Motor Company assembly line 112 years ago. Taylor's idea was to make every step along the assembly line more efficient and effective. No more guess work. The "one best way" became the mantra. And the Model T Ford was the first successful product of scientific management.

Scientific management is based on a simple principle. Workers are more productive when they are assigned narrow and clearly defined tasks. Creativity and guess work are removed. Taylor believed that productivity improved by eliminating unnecessary effort.

In 1908, the Model T Ford was priced at $825 and initially sold well over 10,000 cars.

When Taylor—the first and perhaps the most influential management consultant—came on the scene, he formed his management theories in his best-selling book, *The Principles of Scientific Management*.[1] The book, published in 1911 is still selling like hot cakes on Amazon with a four-and-a-half star rating. Taylor's ideas grabbed Henry Ford's attention. Observing Ford's workers, Taylor considered the most efficient and time-saving methods for increasing the production of the Model T Ford. After a few years, the application of his scientific management principles reduced the average production time of a car to 93 minutes. The sales price dropped to $575. And by 1914, Ford captured 48 percent of the automobile market.[2]

Fast forward 100 years. Most industries still adopt scientific management principles like those used on Ford's assembly line. Although the world of work has profoundly changed, we still use the same systems to manage the production of goods and services. The application of scientific management isn't isolated to the manufacturing sector. They have been applied across the board, including service industries. Telemarketers are given a script to read. Franchise food outlets are based on a system that entrepreneurs pay millions of dollars to purchase. Five-star hotels are run by a procedure's manual. Most successful businesses apply scientific management principles.

Modern jobs, like those on the Ford assembly line, are a series of tasks broken into bite-sized pieces. Jobholders are trained and expected to follow set procedures—they mustn't deviate from the prescribed system. Scientific management isn't confined to blue-collar jobs. Patients are processed through the hospital system. Loan applicants are handled by the bank in a particular way. Job applicants are administered by a recruitment and selection process. Jobholders are appraised and rewarded based on their willingness to follow the system.

The *system* reduces the margin of error. The *system* reduces training costs. The *system* reduces rework. The *system* reduces pay rates. It's little wonder it's still popular, at least with employers. Many employees enjoy the safety of the boundaries that scientific management offers. They don't have to think or take risks. They don't have to reinvent the wheel. They don't have to be creative. Scientific management principles follow the employee through their organizational journey, from starting to parting a company.

A person is hired based on their experience, having demonstrated their willingness to follow the system in other companies. That same person gets a pay-rise on proving their reliability to pursue the company's systems and processes. He or she is trained to learn how to apply the systems in their work. They are appraised once or twice a year on whether their key performance indicators (KPIs) have been achieved. Sometimes people are sacked for deviating from the system.

Scientific management worked well in a stable and predictable world.

But we're no longer living and working in a stable and predictable world. As I illustrate some of the big changes in the past decade in Chapter 1, the world is now in a state of flux. There's little that's stable and predictable in the past decade. In the post-COVID world, it's certain that this volatility will continue.

In a volatility, uncertainty, complexity, and ambiguity (VUCA) world thinking on your feet is the new normal. Thinking laterally and creatively is more valuable than adhering stringently to systems, processes, and procedures. Even so, being creative is risky business. In our paint by numbers workplace, given a choice between following a designated pathway and being unorthodox, most employees will play it safe and not chance their arm. Although it's perceived as the safest route, it's not always the best route. Just like the Ford Motor Company assembly line, employees are clustered into functional specialties, with procedures to follow.

There's discord between the rhetoric and the routine. The mantra is: be innovative and creative. But the practice is to follow standard operating procedures. People are confused. So, the less dangerous path is to follow the *one best way*.

We are seeing gradual improvement. But HR practices are still rooted in procedure. The recruitment and selection process requires interviewers to ask the same questions of each candidate around job competencies. New employees are passive recipients of a generic information dump during their induction. It's one-way traffic from the organization to the individual. The employee is given a piece of paper called a job description that defines their job role, KPIs, and targets. Most of their training is confined to improving technical capabilities. Pay-rises are granted for moving into management. People are appraised on how closely they follow their job specification. Although we've tinkered with these practices, they're still centered on the tenets of scientific management.

The world has moved on, however. Fresh thinking about how we manage people at work is needed.

I use the assembly line analog to structure *The Future of Human Resources*. But it's not an assembly line of production. It's an assembly line of the phases an employee pass through in their employment from starting to parting a company.

In other words, it's the process the employee goes through with an employer. These stages of the process are the familiar touchpoints HR has the most impact over the employee. I'm proposing a makeover of the employee lifecycle, like Taylor did on the Ford assembly line. We examine the major HR practices from organizational entry to exit.

How can these practices be improved? What needs consideration in a climate of accelerated change and uncertainty? How can HR be transformed post-COVID, where all the rules are broken? The central idea of *The Future of Human Resources* is the imperative for HR to adopt an employee-centered approach. By critiquing the employee's organizational journey, the aim is to cultivate the right environment for the employee and their employer to prosper in the post-COVID world.

HR has its finger in many pies. But the pie where it has the greatest influence is the employee lifecycle. We know that generally engagement levels are low. Uncertainty is high. Stress is prevalent. Mental health and well-being are focal points. Competition is heightened. Businesses are looking for better ways to get the best from the people they employ. Employees, particularly younger employees, are searching for meaning in their work. These factors can be considered through the prism of the employee journey through the firm.

Now is a good opportunity for HR to reinvent itself.

My hope is that this book is a catalyst for change. I want to provoke discussion on how HR remains relevant and adds value in the transformative world of work. To make change, we need to think differently; to challenge ourselves not to accept conventional practice. Adopting an employee-centered approach is a good place to start considering the way we approach HR. *The Future of Human Resources* is designed to be a blueprint for change.

The framework I use is the pathway employees walk in their organizational journey. There are four phases to the employee lifecycle. The starting phase is when they commence employment in a new organization. This is followed by the developing phase. This phase assists the employee to grow and develop to be more effective in their current and future job roles. There is the rewarding phase. This phase covers monetary and nonmonetary measures to reward the employee for the work they do. And finally, there's the parting phase where an employee decides to move on from their current employer. Each of these four phases are established, familiar to all employees, and will remain relevant to the employee experience. There are several HR practices that support each phase.

We consider each of the four phases and critically review the supporting HR practices. Although these four phases will stay constant, how they are managed will be scrutinized. The focus is how HR can be reimagined, in other words. These practices are deeply rooted in scientific management. Although scientific management has worked well in the past, it's time to rethink these principles.

It's the perfect time for reflection and renewal as we emerge from the pandemic. Although there is evidence that the changes I am suggesting are occurring in some companies, many businesses are taking tentative steps in the right direction. I will share some successful innovations companies around the world are making. This will hopefully provide you with the confidence to continue the transformation journey.

PART 1 puts the case for change. We look at the changing world of work and map out the necessary mindset shifts. These shifts are opposite to the practices used for a century. These traditional practices have served industry well. But it's time to let go of them and embrace new perspectives. To continue to add value, I argue that HR needs fresh thinking. There are 13 mindset shifts I urge you to consider. During PART 1, I also introduce you to the employee lifecycle framework. This framework provides the structure for implementing these changes.

PART 2 examines the starting phase of employment. Specifically, I look at the recruitment and selection process, induction, working remotely, and the changing expectations managers and employees have of each other in the employment relationship.

PART 3 focuses on the developing phase of employment. In this phase, we look at the obsolete job description. The job description isn't an adequate method for capturing all that the employee is expected to do in the modern workplace. The increasingly important value of nonjob roles is discussed. I also challenge the job design framework we refer to as job specification. We consider a new model of multidimensional learning and development (L&D), to replace the old functional training model. Although job crafting is slow to take hold, it's now time to embrace it to strengthen job specification, the traditional job design mechanism. And finally in this phase, we consider the role of Artificial Intelligence (AI) and smart machines in the workplace. Instead of viewing machines as a competitor for jobs, we need to view AI as a collaborator in super team structures.

PART 4 considers the rewarding phase of employment. Rewarding people for their technical knowhow rather than their people skills must change. Developing performance rather fixating on appraising performance is a shift necessary in the new world of work. Using reward and punishment doesn't ignite human spirit and work. Intrinsic motivation is the driver for success.

And in PART 5, we discussed the inevitable parting phase of employment. I use the word *parting* rather than *exiting* deliberately. By parting, there is a pragmatic acknowledgment that this departure may not necessarily be permanent. We need to leave the door open for departing employees to return either on a part-time, project, or on a full-time basis in the future. If business changes its attitude about the way an employee leaves an organization, it keeping the door open for future employment opportunities.

Finally, I provide 65 questions for you to evaluate your organization against these 13 mindset shifts. You can then build an action plan for making the changes needed.

This book is designed to challenge the conventional thinking about employment. Further, it's a blueprint for HR professionals to make the essential changes to accommodate a new mentality. By making these shifts, HR will continue to add value as a key internal service provider. As we emerge from the constraints of COVID, it's a perfect opportunity to look in the mirror and consider the way we have done things in the past and how we can do things better in the future.

Enjoy.

PART 1

Employee-Centered Approach

CHAPTER 1

The Changing World of Work

As a survival mechanism, employees exercised agility during 2020. The challenge is to maintain this agility while the business recovers to full profitability.

AstraZeneca is an organization that capitalized on employee potential. It was quick to mobilize resources to meet the pressing need to develop a COVID-19 vaccine. Tonya Villafana, AstraZeneca's vice president and global franchise head of infection, credits the company's accelerated response to its ability to tap into a varied pool of experts, both across the company and through its collaboration with the University of Oxford. What's more, AstraZeneca not only involved top experts, but also added high performers who were really passionate and wanted to get involved with the vaccine development team.

"They were the right people at the right time to put into that role. Not everyone has to be an infectious disease expert. It was more about having that kind of passion to deliver and the energy to want to do it."

AstraZeneca also tapped into the potential of its ecosystem. United by a common purpose, the company collaborated with academia and regulatory agencies and applied new ways of working that allowed them to begin vaccine trials in record time, doing in weeks and months what might have taken months four years in the past. The success of those collaborations leads to meaningful change moving forward.[1]

In the past decade, the world has experienced dramatic political, social, technological, scientific, and economic disruption, capped off by the pandemic in 2020. In the early part of 2010–2020, we were recovering from the global fiscal crisis of 2007–2008.

Let me remind you of some of the events in the past decade. From royal weddings to missing planes, there were a plethora of history-defining moments in the second decade of the 21st century. Prince William and Prince Harry's royal weddings, al-Qaeda and Islamic State of Iraq and Syria (ISIS) terror leaders killed, missing Malaysian planes, legalization of same-sex marriage, reality star Donald Trump becoming president, and tech diversity, are just some of the momentous happenings we experienced since 2010.

More specifically, Apple released the world's first iPad, the game-changing piece of technology on April 3, 2010. The South Korean pop superstar *Psy* created Gangnam Style, which became the first video in YouTube's history to reach one billion views in 2012. The world said goodbye on December 05, 2013 to Nelson Mandela, the former president of South Africa and the country's first black head of state. Described as being one of the biggest aviation mysteries in history, MH370, the Malaysian Airlines plane with 239 passengers and crew on board completely vanished on March 08, 2014. The year 2014 was a disastrous one for Malaysian Airlines. Just four months after MH370 went missing, MH17 was shot down while flying over eastern Ukraine, killing all 283 passengers and 15 crew. There was the rise and fall of ISIS. Brutally graphic beheadings, horrific attacks, and suicide bombings from the ISIS hit the western world during its peak in 2015. While the jihadi group-who controlled a population of 8 million at its height-may have been the most powerful and wealthiest force. The ISIS caliphate dream collapsed mid-2017.

The world struck a deal on climate change, dubbed the Paris Agreement, in 2016, dealing with greenhouse gas emissions mitigation, adaptation, and finance. In a history-defining moment on June 26, 2015, the United States legalized same-sex marriage across all 50 states. Ireland, Finland, Greenland, Colombia, Malta, Australia, Germany, Austria, Taiwan, and Ecuador all followed. Greece became the first developed country to default the International Monetary Fund in 2015, which alongside the European Union, provided the nation with €110 billion in loans over three years.

The Brexit Referendum took place. As 52 percent of Britain voted to leave the European Union in 2016, the political debate is still rife. Donald Trump became U.S. president. The television personality, real estate developer, writer, entrepreneur, and investor added another profession to his name in 2016—the 45th President of the United States. There was the largest women's march in history. After just one day of Donald Trump's presidency, more than 5 million people marched globally protesting for women's rights in January 2017. The #MeToo movement started. It became viral on social media following public sexual abuse allegations against Hollywood producer Harvey Weinstein in October 2017. The inspiring campaign led to global awareness, going down as an iconic feminist movement.

The rise of the share economy began. While companies such as Uber and Airbnb were technically founded in 2009 and 2008 respectively, the past 10 years saw the boom in the share economy's popularity. The tech giant, Apple, became the first public company to be worth US$1 trillion in 2018. The first photo of a black hole was taken. Astronomers captured the awe-inspiring sight on April 10, 2019, making it one of the biggest space moments in recent history. These are just a few of the events in the past 10 years.[2]

The world of work has been in a constant state of upheaval too, like most aspects of life. After the 2020 pandemic we all yearn for a period of stability. But we need to accept that disruption and dislocation is now part of "normal" life. This is the new reality.

Is HR Ready?

Surveys show that HR enhanced its reputation in the way it dealt with the COVID crisis.[3] HR is in a great position to capitalize on its new status. But if we dig a little deeper, it's the traditional domains of HR that get high marks. Executives praise HR for its handling of health and safety matters, its workforce communication strategies, and promoting the well-being of employees. HR now needs to expand its influence in other areas.

If we assume that disruption is now the constant (and this is a fair assumption), HR must adjust. While keeping its good reputation in customary areas, tackling some of the other issues affecting employee performance is the next frontier. I will discuss these in the following chapter.

Before we consider these HR issues, let's consider some of the broad strategic issues for business.

The first obvious adjustment is that conventional strategic planning isn't viable anymore. As a replacement, companies need to focus finding a value-based purpose in a turbulent and unpredictable marketplace. Values are enduring. Strategic plans are not. Values offer a foundation to build upon. But a strategic plan can be obsolete by the time the ink has dried. A values-based purpose gives the business scope to pivot in unforeseen circumstances. Values supply guiding principles for clarity of direction. For instance, *being flexible and innovative*, suggests that the business should change when the opportunity arises. *Being customer-focused* remind the business of its #1 priority, regardless of fluctuations in the marketplace. Short-term goals can be shaped around values.

There are two types of values. A value can be terminal or instrumental. In his book, *The Nature of Human Values*,[4] social psychologist Milton Rokeach defines the difference between terminal and instrumental values. Rokeach defines values as, "enduring beliefs that a specific mode of conduct or end-state of existence is personally or socially preferable to an opposite or converse mode of conduct or end-state of existence." Terminal values signify a destination or outcome. Instrumental values signify a behavior.

Let's look at some illustrations of terminal and instrumental values in a business context. Terminal values provide a direction for the future. For example, terminal values include:

- Profitability
- Quality
- Excellence

On the other hand, instrumental values might include:

- Taking responsible risks
- Innovating
- Continuous improvement
- Being a "team player"

Instrumental values are generally a guide to acceptable behavior that is observable.

In a climate of accelerated change and uncertainty, specific goals can become obsolete quickly in changing circumstances that can't be predicted. Values are enduring and more reliable indications in the face of ambiguity.

For HR, setting a clear set of values that are both terminal and instrumental would be a good place to start. I'm hoping that the 13 mindset shifts I introduce in Chapter 5 will give you a basis for formulating a new set of values consistent with these transformations.

Ken Sneader and Bob Sternfels of McKinsey in their article, *From Surviving to Thriving: Reimagining the Post-COVID-19 Return*,[5] suggest that to come back stronger, companies should reimagine their business model as they return to full speed. They identify four areas to focus on: recovering revenue, rebuilding operations, rethinking the organization, and accelerating the adoption of digital solutions. For businesses to rethink their operating model, HR must adapt too.

As a survival mechanism, employees exercised agility during 2020. The challenge is to maintain this agility while the business recovers to full profitability. Undoubtedly, there are lessons to be learned from the pandemic. What were the success factors that facilitated this agility?

Where the Rubber Meets the Road

A Lesson in Agility and Responsiveness

Consider a Chinese car-rental company whose revenues fell 95 percent in February 2020. With the roads empty, company leaders didn't just stew. Instead, they reacted like a start-up. They invested in micro-customer segmentation and social listening to guide personalization. This led them to develop new use cases. They discovered, for example, that many tech firms were telling employees not to use public transportation. The car-rental company used this insight to experiment with and refine targeted campaigns. They also called first-time customers who had canceled orders to reassure them of the various safety steps the company had taken, such as "no touch" car pickup. To manage the program, they pulled together three agile teams with cross-functional skills and designed a recovery dashboard to track progress. Before the crisis, the company took up to three weeks to launch a campaign; that is now down to two to three days. Within seven weeks, the company had recovered 90 percent of its business, year on year—almost twice the rate of its chief competitor (Sneader and Sternfels 2020).[6]

Agility

Agility can mean many things. It's a word we tossed around before the pandemic. In the context of speed in a crisis, it means putting into place new operating models that focus on the end-user, the customer, supported by rigorous processes. Being able to be responsive and pivot quickly is critical to success in a post-COVID marketplace, as it was during the peak of the pandemic. Operationally, it means accelerating end-to-end value chain digitalization. Digitalization tools are available, and they can significantly reduce the cost of flexibility. Low-cost and flexible operating systems are not only now possible, but they are also available. The challenge for HR is how they can synchronize people with these tools to provide speed and precision. The benefits are higher productivity, more flexibility, enhanced quality, and more customer connectivity. I discuss this further in Chapter 14.

Undoubtedly, the future of work involves more automation and use of technology. The pandemic has hastened the pace. Working remotely, employees across all functions of the business have learned how to complete tasks, using digital communication and collaboration tools. With increased technology, we're seeing humans doing less manual and repetitive tasks. And this means that employees are doing more analytical and technical support work. As Sneader and Sternfels of McKinsey point out, "This shift will call for substantial investment in workforce engagement and training in new skills, much of it delivered using digital tools." They're right and we should prepare for this if we haven't already.

Matching talent with agile practices is challenging. Hierarchy and past performance can be roadblocks. Simplifying and streamlining organizational structures, centered around project-based teams is required. Aptitude and getting results are now more valuable than expertise and experience. Developing leaders shouldn't be confined to the hierarchical positioning of people. Leaders can emerge from everywhere in the structure. Leadership development programs should be more dynamic. A renewed emphasis on talent development will help to attract and retain top talent.

Digital communication is now commonplace. During 2020, there was a transformation in the way we interactive with one another. It wasn't just the way we communicated with work colleagues, but in some cases our loved ones, and with suppliers of specialist services, such as medical care, and routine transactions. The pandemic has accelerated the migration to digital communication technologies. This will surely be a turning point in history. We need to accept that remote working in some form, probably in a hybrid format as I suggest in Chapter 8, is likely to be continued well after the pandemic has passed.

As we move back to full recovery, some fundamental communication changes will need to be addressed. Consumers now are connecting with businesses in many more ways than previously. Businesses need to be geared up for all the access channels customers elect to use with businesses.

In the next chapter, we look at some of the big HR issues and how this shapes their services.

Ten Key Takeaways

1. In the past decade, the world has experienced dramatic political, social, technological, scientific, and economic disruption, capped off by the pandemic in 2020.
2. The world of work has been in a constant state of upheaval too, like most aspects of life.
3. Surveys show that HR enhanced its reputation in the way it dealt with the COVID crisis. HR is in a great position to capitalize on its new status.
4. If we assume that disruption is now the constant (and this is a fair assumption), HR must adjust.
5. The first obvious adjustment is that conventional strategic planning isn't viable anymore.
6. As a replacement, companies need to focus finding a value-based purpose in a turbulent and unpredictable marketplace.
7. In a climate of accelerated change and uncertainty, specific goals can become obsolete quickly in changing circumstances that can't be predicted.
8. Companies should reimagine their business model as they return to full speed.
9. Matching talent with agile practices is challenging.
10. Digital communication is now commonplace.

CHAPTER 2

A World Without Work?

Machines don't need to be human to be as effective as a human.

One thing is clear looking ahead, it's this: work as we know it will never be the same again. With every rule book thrown out thanks to the COVID-19 pandemic, 2021 is the year of possibilities. There's never been a better time to head back to the drawing board and take a chance on big ideas.[1]

The old cliché, that *employees are our greatest asset*, is more relevant today than at any time since the *Industrial Revolution*. Why? All businesses have access to the same technology. They have access to the same processes and procedures. They have access to the same suppliers that support the business. So, the competitive advantage is still the people who are employed in the business. AI he's challenging this assertion. But in a VUCA world, it's people that can (at least for the foreseeable future) navigate through the terrain.

A dominant debate over the past decade has been whether AI will eventually replace people. Will this result in fewer jobs, or even a world without jobs? Most economists argue that AI will create jobs, at least at the rate that they are lost to AI. In other words, a pool of jobs will exist, except that they will be different. That sounds mildly reassuring.

But Oxford Professor Daniel Susskind breaks rank with his latest book, *A World Without Work*. He argues very thoroughly and convincingly that it's only a matter of time before machines created a world without work. Susskind states that, "the demand for the work of human beings is likely to wither away, gradually."[2] His arguments for this are very compelling, quite frankly.

World Without Work?

There is an emerging school of thought that there won't be enough work. The conventional wisdom is that as new technology develops it will displace workers rather than replace them. New technology will create new work opportunities. This is a comforting image of the future, far more comforting than the idea of a world without work! Susskind details how machines and AI will increasingly master tasks and activities that, until recently, humans thought they alone could undertake. From diagnosing mental conditions and designing skyscrapers to composing music and reporting the news, Susskind argues that technology is taking over existing jobs faster than humans can create new ones.

He explains that jobs are a cluster of small tasks. And that more and more tasks are being done by machines, eventually to a point where people only perform a few of those tasks. What's more, it's misleading to think that because machines can't think like humans, there will always be work tasks for humans.

But machines don't need to think like humans to be better than humans in those tasks. For example, machines are better at diagnosing illnesses than specialist doctors. This is because the machine can access and process literally billions of cases in a short amount of time. The machine can give a diagnosis from "experience." They can analyze emotions via facial expressions and then respond accordingly in "interpersonal" encounters. So, machines don't need to be human to be as effective as a human.

So, if we thought COVID-19 sent shockwaves through global labor markets, the idea of a world without work is a sobering thought for all of us. "The past year has demonstrated that many so-called face-to-face jobs—those of lawyers, doctors, and teachers—can actually be undertaken in concert with machines."[3] Susskind expands: "Overnight, things like telemedicine, virtual courts, and online education became the norm. And people are, by and large, happy with machines playing a larger role" (Stapleton 2021).[4]

Most economists still believe that "technological unemployment" doesn't lead to a permanent net loss of jobs in capitalist societies. Instead, technology unemployment frees up the workforce to take on new tasks, improve overall productivity, an increase our prosperity. But Susskind differs from this conventional view. He thinks it's a mistake to draw lessons from the past for the future of work.

Although none of us really know what the future holds, what are the implications for HR? We can only foresee what's going to happen short term. It's obvious that human beings working and interacting with machines is only going to increase. This trend will continue. Therefore, HR's role, for several years to come, must evolve into one of cultivating collaboration between human work and machine work. So, it's the interaction between machines and people that needs to become a focal point for HR in the short term. What happens after that is anybody's guess.

In practice, HR must provide training and development opportunities to use emerging technology and budget accordingly for the future. This has implications beyond L&D. For instance, it will affect recruitment and selection and the management of performance. The potential for humans to interact with machines will increasingly be considered as a criterion in the selection process. It also means that performance will be measured by the capacity of the employee to work collaboratively with AI. I have more to say about these implications in Chapter 14.

In the short-to-medium future, the question for HR is: How can AI and employees coexist for the mutual betterment of business and people? We are well past the either/or argument; that is, people versus machines. Machines are pervasively encroaching on every side of our lives and permanently. They are pervading everything we do for one reason: smart machines add value. Machines can do routine tasks faster, cheaper, and more accurately than humans.

If machines can do things quicker, with less errors, more cost-effectively, and better than we humans, they get a ticket to the dance, in our place. We need to be clear-eyed about this. At least for now, it's the relationship between people and AI that holds the key to business success. As Professor David Autor, co-chair of MIT taskforce on the work of the future puts it, people tended to "overstate the extent of machine substitution for human labor and ignore the strong complementarities between automation and labor."[5] So, it's not a question of whether machines will replace humans, at least in the short term. It's more useful to ask how AI and people can continue to interact to produce better products and services. HR undoubtedly has a key role to play in enabling this continual interaction between employees and new technologies.

Technology, and its inevitable progress to make things better, faster, more cost effective, and easier is critical for business success. Technological advancement is unavoidable. I think it's something to be fully embraced and to be excited about. Our focus now is how humans and AI can collaborate even more effectively. It's the cooperation between people and technology that ultimately provides the post-COVID business with a competitive edge.

Where the Rubber Meets the Road

Evie the AI Virtual Personal Assistant

Evie, the virtual personal assistant, was so professional and personable when scheduling meetings that many users never doubted "she" was not a real human being. People thanked "her" personally and asked to see "her" in person at meetings. Once, a conference organizer even prepared an access pass for "her," believing "she" would be attending the event. One popular technology publication considered Evie such an affordable service that it was touted as "a personal assistant for the 99%." Its creator, Evie.ai, a Singapore-based AI company, was ranked as one of the top startups to watch in 2017. (Joseph, Lim, and Chun 2018)[6]

Agility Is the New Black

But the ability to be agile, to pivot rapidly, and consider things from diverse angles are things humans do better, at least for the near future. As we saw during COVID-19, these traits are necessary, not only to survive but also to thrive in a VUCA landscape. Other crises await. And we need to be able to respond.

During 2020, with COVID-19 in full rage, organizations were forced to adopt radically new ways of working and running. Flying by the seat of your pants was given a whole new meaning. This incremental approach was born out of necessity. Responding quickly and changing direction was stimulated by a pandemic, with all the local and global human and economic reverberations. The volatile nature of the pandemic confounded efforts to predict and plan with any certainty and precision.

Businesses had to respond (we all did) to a crisis we'd never encountered. Prior to COVID, popular management books had been promoting agility as the new black. So was I. Agility being now the new black, instead of talking about it—as if a new fad—business now applies it to everything it says, thinks, and does. The year 2020 and the aftermath has tested conventional thinking. It's not just our thinking that's been challenged, it's everything we do.

For example, we now spend time checking into places such as restaurants and leaving our details. We now need to take our masks, as well as our car keys, wallets, and phone with us when leaving our homes. The pandemic challenges the way we interacted with one another. We now indulge in a glut of zoom calls, instead of meeting in the corridor. With new vaccines, this pandemic will (hopefully) eventually disappear. Fingers crossed. But the way we work and live has changed forever.

Agility was highly valued and needed during the pandemic. Thinking with agility is distinctly human, at least for now. The circumstances of 2020 required this type of thinking. It forced us to work differently. The questions raised and the decisions made were made by humans, not machines. Courage, judgment, resilience, and flexibility are human traits that took center stage in a crisis. Humans and their ability to be human, was crucial for business survival.

Compared with the pandemic, our pre-COVID world was predictable and steady. In a durable and inevitable environment, machines rule. Standard processes and procedures can be governed by technology. Big data reigns supreme. But we've also rediscovered that humanness has significant advantages. The challenge now for HR is how these advantages can be harnessed more fully and embedded in the employee experience at work. How can agile thinking be used in tandem with technology?

Being human is in vogue again, for the moment.

Contingency Work

It's not just work that's changing, but the type of employment. How can we address the issue of the rise of part-time work, for instance? As Sophie Deutsch, a journalist writing for *HRM*, an Australia-based online

HR magazine, observes, "We've been waving goodbye to the nine-to-five grind from Monday-Friday for some time now ..."[7] For some time now there's a consistent trend toward part-time or contingency work.

The rise of part-time work is undoubtedly a desire to exercise choice and more control over one's career. People want the flexibility contingency work offers to balance their home and work lives. Part-time work gives people more options.

Opportunities for part-time work will vary from industry to industry. For instance, the hospitality and age care industries are two that have seen a significant growth in contingency work opportunities. More broadly, as service industries continue to dominate the economy, it's where more part-time work prospects will flourish.

What's more, the acceleration of contingency work has been exacerbated by COVID-19. Industries most vulnerable during COVID-19 were able to survive by moving to a part-time work model. The arts, tourism, and hospitality are three industries severely affected during the pandemic. And many workers were forced to move to part-time working arrangements if they were lucky to have a job at all. Many people took on several part-time jobs to survive during this period. This trend will undoubtedly endure.

What are the implications for employees and employers?

The employer–employee relationship changes by the aggregated percentage of contingency workers. Instead of being invested with one boss, more people are taking the initiative and looking after their own job security by having several part-time jobs. If one freelance job disappears, the contingency worker has got the security of another part-time role. Managers therefore don't have the same control that they had with a full-time employee that's entirely dependent on one source of income. I discuss this evolving employment relationship in Chapter 9.

Another implication is that this move to contingency work places more pressure on companies to offer flexible working arrangements for their employees. These adaptable arrangements include reduced hours, shared jobs, and more remote employment opportunities, to name a few.

Employers need a different mindset to accommodate these inevitable employment trends. For instance, PwC's study of 32,500 participants from 19 countries, including more than 2,000 Australians, found that

90 percent of Australians want to work from home in some capacity (Deutsch 2021).[8] This trend means company offices will be more collaborative places in the office, with less fixed desks, and more mobile workspaces. The work itself will need redesigning to accommodate this move to a more mobile workforce. Jobs will be flexible, adaptable, and adjusted to the needs of the jobholder.

Job sharing is on the rise. As we know, it's becoming an increasingly acceptable practice for two applicants to join forces to apply for one role. For job sharing to work, there's a need for a constructive working relationship between the two jobholders. This can be a challenge. Communication is paramount. The other challenge for the employer is when one of those two people decides to quit. How are these circumstances managed?

HR need to acknowledge, prepare, and respond to our changing world and its impact on work. We looked at the inevitable rise of AI and its uneasy rivalry with humans for organizational work. The pandemic renewed the value and importance of the human trait for agile thinking. The challenge for the future is how agility can be applied. Finally, we discussed the rise of contingency work and its implications for employers and employees.

In the next chapter, I look at the three drivers for the 13 mindset shifts I discuss in PARTS 2, 3, and 4: purpose, potential, and perspective.

Ten Key Takeaways

1. The old cliché, that *employees are our greatest asset*, is more relevant today than at any time since the Industrial Revolution.
2. A dominant debate over the past decade has been whether AI will eventually replace people.
3. Daniel Susskind argues that it's only a matter of time before machines created a world without work.
4. Most economists still believe that "technological unemployment" doesn't lead to a permanent net loss of jobs in capitalist societies.
5. In the short-to-medium future, the question for HR is: How can AI and employees coexist for the mutual betterment of business and people?

6. The ability to be agile, to pivot rapidly, and consider things from diverse angles are things humans do well.
7. The rise of part-time work is undoubtedly a desire to exercise choice and more control over one's career.
8. The acceleration of contingency work has been exacerbated by COVID-19.
9. The employer–employee relationship changes by the aggregated percentage of contingency workers.
10. Another implication is that this move to contingency work places more pressure on companies to offer flexible working arrangements for their employees.

CHAPTER 3

Employee Purpose, Potential, and Perspective

Past performance doesn't predict untapped future experiences.

Payment's technology company MasterCard exemplifies how a deeper understanding of worker potential can help inform workforce planning and development efforts. With rapid growth, MasterCard business and HR leaders realized that the organization needed a clear understanding of its workforce's skills and capabilities, especially considering technology-driven change. To clarify how roles and skills were changing as technology evolves, the organization invested in AI to model emerging technologies impact on any economy, industry, organization, or job.

During the pandemic, this platform had been key in guarding some decisions on work flexibility ranges. In the future, the organization plans to use the insights from this tool to guide day-to-day learning investments and, ultimately, support worker career progression. This analytics-driven approach has moved MasterCard beyond the traditional approach of identifying employee profiles from the top down and matching them with training needs.

Instead, the technology infers employee profiles from the bottom up by analyzing multiple large scale data sets from many systems and sources (such as performance management, job descriptions, learning management systems, and career conversations). This allows MasterCard to more accurately understand its workers skills to identify organization-wide strengths and development areas. (Deloitte Insights 2021)[1]

In this chapter, I want to discuss the high-level drivers that support the mindset shifts we'll cover shortly. Deloitte's 2021 global human capital trends report[2] neatly summarizes three drivers for the future of HR as *purpose*, *potential*, and *perspective*. Purpose is people first, focusing on the employee and their organizational journey. Potential refers to looking more dynamically at what people are capable of, instead of embracing the familiar cliché that the *past predicts the future*. It's time to adopt a more optimistic and less limiting view of human nature. Can we reasonably predict people's potential? Absolutely. Past behavior predicts future success only in what people have experienced. Earlier experience doesn't, however, predict opportunities. Assessing people's capabilities by what they have done is redundant in a world of future uncertainty. And perspective means challenging of old beliefs and practices. It centers on trusting that employees will grow and develop without the barriers of past conformity practices. The new perspective means letting go of scientific management conventions such as job specification, performance reviews, and other practices.

These three drivers aren't ideals without a practical application—they represent imperatives for the changing world of work. They also supply the context for *The Future of Human Resources*. In other words, the three drivers are the themes supporting the mindset shifts we cover.

Looking back, HR has been too preoccupied with processes, procedures, methods, and systems. This isn't just my observation. It's the perception of many line managers and team members, even some who work in HR. And perception is reality in the eyes of the observers. Systemization is, of course, part of HR's business. But it's certainly not where it adds value. Being wedded to systemization diminishes the profession for those it serves, the internal customer.

People First

As I said in the introduction, adopting an employee-centered approach is now the way forward.

For the past 100 years, our workplaces have been progressively dehumanized. I discuss the dehumanization of work in my book, *Bringing the*

Human Being Back to Work: The 10 Performance and Development Conversations Leaders Must Have.[3] We've lost sight of an organization, any organization, being a bunch of people working toward a common goal. This simple idea seems to have got lost in the quest to systemize businesses. COVID-19 has reminded us, albeit, in a painful way, of the value human beings bring to the workplace.

We've become obsessed at performance managing employees, rather than developing people. Employees submit to a job specification and a job description and are rated and scaled at appraisal time. Employees are expected to follow instructions, hit their KPIs, and not upset the applecart. Despite the rhetoric to the contrary, people are categorized, labeled, and processed as resources. They are small cogs in a large wheel of production.

Is it any surprise that most people are disengaged in their work? It shouldn't be.

We still label people at work as human capital, or worse a human resource; these labels dehumanize people and turn them into an abstract piece of machinery. A human resource is lumped in with technical, administrative, and financial resources. People are expected to leave their humanness at the door of the business and become compliant to conduct predetermined business outcomes.

Am I being too harsh? I think not.

The business world over the past century has increasingly become a cold, clinical, rational place. HR, which has developed into an industry, has complicated things in its attempt to legitimize its existence. We've downsized, upsized, and rightsized the workforce. We've got function-based work, project-based work, KPIs, key result areas (KRAs), and so on. It's time for HR to lead a people first agenda.

It's timely to rethink the fundamental driver of HR success. My mission is to bring the human beings back to work before the machines take over. Just kidding! Although Daniel Susskind, in the last chapter, believes this is what awaits us.

How can we put people in the driving seat rather than the back seat? How can we adopt an employee-centric focus?

By employee centric, I'm not arguing that HR should become a de facto union. Getting the best from people, by unlocking their potential, is in sync with business success. I'd suggest HR's role is to create an environment where people can give their best willingly. And I believe that the COVID crisis gives us a wonderful opportunity to rethink the charter and direction of HR.

The world we live in is so radically different, even in the past decade, as I illustrated in Chapter 2. Things are changing around us so quickly it's hard for us to step back and see the magnitude of the transformation. One thing is certain: Change will continue and accelerate. We need to adapt and be responsive to these transformations. The nature of work is radically different from Henry Ford's assembly line.

Even though work has transformed, most of our systems, processes, and procedures are based on scientific management philosophy. How can we empower people and engage them in the work they do? How can we change the way people are led at work? What can leaders do (and not do) to make the necessary changes? What and where are the roadblocks? These are the big questions I want to explore in the coming chapters.

I should point out that the answer isn't necessarily about being kind, gentle, and caring. Although I'm sure you'd agree, more of that wouldn't go astray! There's a pragmatic edge to my message. I want people to give more of themselves at work. You do too. Surely. The aim must be to ignite people's human spirit in the organizational work they do. Human enterprise—the kind we saw during the pandemic—is missing in workplaces across the globe.

People are trained to act like machines in the workplace, with minimal free will or enterprise. And from what we're being told, machines will eventually replace people. That's ironic. We need to reinvent what it means to be human in the context of work.

Where the Rubber Meets the Road

Adrenaline Shot of Engagement

Organizations are spending hundreds of millions of dollars on employee engagement programs, yet their scores on engagement surveys remain abysmally low. How is that possible? Because most initiatives amount to an adrenaline shot. A perk is introduced to boost scores, but over time the effect wears off and scores go back down. Another perk is introduced, and scores go back up—and then they fall again. The more this cycle repeats itself, the more it feels like manipulation.

People begin to recognize the short-term fixes for what they are. When organizations make real gains, it's because they're thinking longer term. They're going beyond what engagement scores are telling them to do in the moment and redesigning employee experience, creating a place where people want, not just need, to work each day. But what does that mean, and what does it look like? (Morgan 2017)[4]

Two Relationships Need to Change

The first relationship in need of an overhaul is between managers and employees. This relationship, the lynchpin of industry, must become less adversarial and more collaborative. The other relationship that needs attention is between the jobholder and their job.

For several decades, the employment relationship has been in transition from the old "them & us" to a more collaborative alliance. The pandemic has hastened this transformation. Traditional managers will, however, be keen to reassert their dominance in the post-COVID era. Likewise, traditional employees in a more certain business landscape will be waiting to return to being issued instructions on what to do. We may be in danger of slowing any momentum to a new employment relationship.

What's more, there are powerful vested interests waiting to stifle a move to a new collaborative working relationship between the manager and employee. Employer groups and trade unions may see it in their interests to support a "them & us" employment relationship.

During remote working arrangements, the manager didn't have the luxury of look over the shoulder of their workers. Regardless of our view about working remotely, this is a trend that will continue. This physical dislocation compels employees to think for themselves more often. It also forces managers to lead differently. These remote working arrangements require more collaboration and less command and control.

What about the relationship between the jobholder and the work they do?

Instead of designing jobs and retrofitting people into those jobs, it's time to redesign jobs that capitalize on the strengths and capabilities of the person doing the work. The job specification has dominated organizational life since the birth of industry. Job specification has its place; its design is to make organizational work more efficient and effective. But it needs less rigidity. Job design can balance efficiency with the needs and interests of the jobholder.

You are aware of the alarmingly low levels of employee engagement. Some surveys rate disengagement as high as 70 percent. Why are people disengaged? I think the answer, which hasn't really been considered in great depth in the leadership literature, is the work itself. We have dumbed down work into its simple component parts just like the Ford assembly line. This reduces training costs, minimizes error rates, and maximized output, but at the excessive cost of disengagement. We need to change our thinking about how we design work. The costs of breaking work down to a paint-by-numbers approach, is now costing more than the savings of job specification.

There are several important messages for HR. I discuss their implications in the pages ahead. But generally, we need to think and act differently. Traditional scientific management principles are no longer serving us well. Fresh perspectives are to be embraced.

We should fully integrate the well-being of employees with their organizational work. Work can be designed with the employees' physical, mental, and social health needs considered. The fundamental question is this: How can work be designed to bring the best out of the person doing the work? The days of moulding the jobholder to fit a rigidly defined job specification is ending. Let's abandon the cookie-cutter approach of fitting people into a job specification.

The relationship of the jobholder and their job should be turned on its head. How can work be changed to accommodate the innate talents, strengths, needs, and preferences of the person doing it? The design of the job influences all HR practices. Recruitment and selection, induction and onboarding, training and development, promotion and succession planning, rewards and remuneration, reviewing performance, and even, exiting and leaving the business are all affected. HR is at the forefront of this change.

Changing the relationship between the jobholder and job through redesigning work will be empowering. The perennial challenge of engaging hearts and minds at work may be partially resolved with more empowerment over the work people do. We've been giving lip service to empowerment for decades. But now we must consider it more deeply than offering free massages and other treats. If businesses want their employees to respond like they did in 2020, they must be given an extended license to exercise prudent independent judgment. Staying flexible and maneuverable in a climate of ambiguity and transformation requires independent judgment and initiative from everyone. As the goal posts continue moving, so do the tactics of the players.

Let's revisit purpose, potential, and perspective. The purpose is a people-first value. That means putting energy into the employee lifecycle I will illustrate in the next chapter. Potential is unleashing the ability of the employee. This starts with revamping the two most significant relationships the employee has at work: with their manager and with their job. And perspective is adopting new approaches that are not grounded in the principles of scientific management. This means backing employees to use and exercise their independent judgment and to show prudent initiative. This is done by providing employees with the tools to be empowered in the work they do. The three drivers supply the narrative for HR for its future direction.

The implications of these issues I raise here affect the work setting and HR. HR has little choice but to change direction. Changing direction needs a change of thinking. Further, this requires HR professionals to let go of past practices and adopt an innovative approach. I think we have been slow to adjust to these evolving trends. The pandemic has raised the stakes, however. Overall, the profession must move from a role of standardizing and enforcing workplace policies to one of facilitating and empowering changes across the enterprise, such as the ones I've discussed. The challenge is for the profession to reinvent itself and communicate its new charter to the web of stakeholders it serves within and outside the organization.

In the next chapter, I introduce you to the employee lifecycle framework. This is the framework I use to guide and inform the 13 mindset shifts we look at in PART 2 and beyond.

Ten Key Takeaways

1. The three drivers for HR are purpose, potential, and perspective.
2. Purpose is people first, focusing on the employee and their organizational journey.
3. Potential refers to looking more dynamically at what people are capable of, instead of embracing the familiar cliché that the past predicts the future.
4. Perspective means challenging old beliefs and practices.
5. HR has been too preoccupied with processes, procedures, methods, and systems.
6. For the past 100 years, our workplaces have been progressively dehumanized.
7. Even though work has transformed, most of our systems, processes, and procedures are based on scientific management philosophy.
8. The first relationship in need of an overhaul is between managers and employees.
9. The second relationship that needs revamping is between the job-holder and the work they do.
10. Purpose, potential, and perspective is the framework used to guide and inform the 13 mindset shifts.

CHAPTER 4

The Employee Lifecycle Framework

An employee is not an asset. It's what the employee can possibly offer that's the asset. It's a person's potential, in other words, that becomes the asset.

Sumeet Shetty, product development manager at SAP India, inherited a new team. Some of the team members were very comfortable—too comfortable—in their routine. They were in a rut. But Shetty saw that they were capable of more.

He decided to give his team stretch assignments. This including an exercise in which team members had to rehearse board report presentations several times. The team members complained that rehearsing for a board presentation was unnecessary. And their first attempts were very poor, reflecting these sentiments. But after several attempts, the presentations were improving.

When the team reported back at the end of the year on Shetty's performance, they cited this stretch assignment as the most impactful thing he had done as a manager. Six months earlier he had been desperate to find a way to stop the whining and complaining. And finding a professional solution was not easy, but ultimately ended up being what they needed (Johnson 2019).[1]

I layout the framework here for rest of the book. This framework is the employee lifecycle. The employee lifecycle names the main phases and practices employees are exposed to from the beginning to the end of their organizational journey. During their working life, the employee as they change employer goes through several cycles of the same framework. These phases and practices stay constant from one employer to the next.

The framework supplies a foundation to explore the issues I raised in the earlier chapters. In PARTS 2, 3, 4, and 5 we examine the transformations necessary for each HR practice. The employee lifecycle framework puts the spotlight squarely on the employee organizational pathway. It's the focus on the employee, and how to create the right environment for them to realize their full potential, which gives HR the blueprint to reinvent itself.

Employees Are Our Greatest Asset

Let's revisit the cliché that *our employees are our greatest asset.* We've heard it so many times that we get blasé about it. Is it true? Are employees really the company's greatest asset? Many employees are very skeptical about this statement, and for good reason. If employees are the greatest asset to an organization, why then does it have to be continually restated in blogs, company websites, financial reports, and everywhere else? Shouldn't it be obvious, if true? It's an easy statement to make. It rolls off the tongue. But the reality is quite different on the ground.

The Korn Ferry Institute, the research arm of the executive search and consulting firm, asked 800 CEOs and other top leaders at global firms about what generates profit for their companies and how workers fit into that vision. Two-thirds said they believe technology will create greater value in the future than their workforce, and 44 percent believe that automation, AI, and robotics will make people "largely irrelevant" in the years to come (Weber 2016).[2]

The research took place several years ago. It's likely that these views will have solidified since these findings. AI hasn't yet made employees irrelevant. Yet we see article-after-article and company website-after-website claiming that it's employees who are our greatest asset. Employees are smart enough to know that there's a whiff of hypocrisy.

The best test of this statement is during hard times. If a company is going through a difficult patch and the first thing it does is offload their employees, this would suggest the statement is untrue, despite the rhetoric. It's common practice for employees to be laid off or receive a pay cut during a downturn in business activity. Other assets such as intellectual property or physical assets often remain at the expense of employees.

Surely if employees were a company's most important asset, this asset would be protected before any other assets? It's little wonder that employees are very cynical about this platitude.

The other problem I have with the term "asset" is this: asset implies, like a liability, that the business *owns* it. In other words, the employee is a business possession, asset or not. And if the business owns the employee, it suggests the company can do what it pleases with employees. The company can off load them. Treat them well. Neglect them. Or treat them poorly. After all, the company has other assets such as machinery, inventory, and technology. And of course, the company can buy and sell those assets and resources too. So, even if employees are a company's greatest asset they can be bought and sold at will.

I think the statement is false. An employee is not an asset. It's what the employee can possibly offer that's the asset. It's a person's potential, in other words, that becomes the asset. When an employee is recruited and selected to fill a vacant or create a new position, they bring with them experience and qualifications. But it's not until they're in the job and adding value to the business that they become an asset. If we're going to classify an employee as an asset, it's no different to purchasing a printer, for example. While a printer might be expensive to purchase and promises to do lots of whiz bang things, it's not until it produces results that we can classify it as an asset to the business.

As we know, performance can vary significantly on the job, for a range of reasons beyond the jobholder's skills and experience. How one performs on the job is the determinant of whether they add value to the business, or not. In other words, it is what people do (or not do) in their work role that counts. Human effort helps an organization achieve its strategic direction. Human effort is what assists (with machines) to produce superior products and services. Human effort produces great marketing campaigns. Human effort creates great teamwork. It's the potential of people that is really the key driver for business success.

HR's primary role is to provide a conducive working environment for employees to flourish. And when they flourish and maximize their potential, they are THEN an asset to the business.

As Anthony Bradley and Mark McDonald state in their Harvard Business Review article, *People Are Not Your Greatest Asset*:

What is the primary purpose of a business organization? To assemble a group of people, who previously may have had no association, and empower them to accomplish productive work toward the organization's objectives.[3]

Providing a great working environment involves a complex array of factors, including the removal of roadblocks. A new employee is usually keen to create a good first impression; they are full of good intentions. The employee is willing to make their contribution and then be an asset to the business. Everyone wants the new employee to succeed. The business also wants them to succeed. Their manager wants them to succeed. HR wants them to succeed. But these well wishes and initial enthusiasm is usually dampened by a range of factors.

So, I think the company's greatest asset is a potential contribution of its employees. The key question then must be: What is HR doing, or not doing, to support the potential contribution of employees? The answer if properly implemented can then go some way to getting the very best from its greatest asset: employee potential.

Where the Rubber Meets the Road

Bullshit Jobs

Do you have a job that you secretly believe is pointless?

If so, you have what anthropologist David Graeber calls a "bullshit job." A professor at the London School of Economics, Graeber has written a new book called *Bullshit Jobs: A Theory*.

He argues that there are millions of people across the world—clerical workers, administrators, consultants, telemarketers, corporate lawyers, service personnel, and many others—who are toiling away in meaningless, unnecessary jobs, and they know it.

It didn't have to be this way, Graeber says. Technology has advanced to the point where most of the difficult, labor-intensive jobs can be performed by machines. But instead of freeing ourselves from the suffocating 40-hour workweek, we've invented a whole universe of futile occupations that are professionally unsatisfying and spiritually empty.[4]

The Employee Lifecycle Framework

To answer this question, let's start with the main touch points HR has with employees.

The following illustration is the employee lifecycle framework.

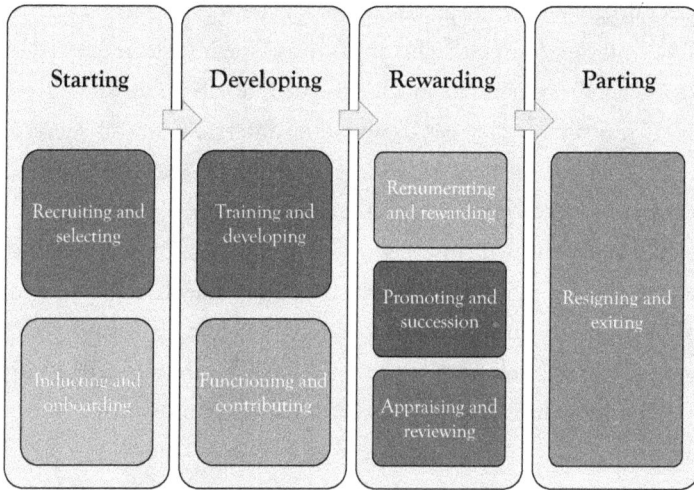

Figure 4.1 Employee lifecycle framework

I've identified the four phases an employee goes through during their employment in any organization. These phases are *starting*, *developing*, *rewarding*, and *parting*. Each phase has its own practices. Although the phases are sequential, the practices in each phase are not necessarily so. But they're nonetheless part of the employee's experience in a workplace.

It's unlikely that these phases and practices will change. They are a constant in the life of any employee in the past and most probably in the future. The framework helps to focus attention on the key touch points HR has with employees throughout their lifecycle.

But it's the eight practices that I will challenge.

I want to question them from several perspectives:

- What is the purpose of the practice?
- What are some diverse ways to consider the effectiveness of the practice?
- What is HR's role in each practice?
- How can they change to better suit the practice?

These are the questions that I am interested in.

So, I will confine my focus to the framework throughout the rest of the book. There are matters requiring the attention of HR beyond the framework. But I believe this framework is the starting point to reinvent HR from the perspective of the employee's organizational journey.

Let's briefly review the phases and practices.

The employee journey begins at the recruitment stage. Interested candidates generally respond to an advertisement or tap on the shoulder and apply. If shortlisted, they get to attend an interview. And if successful, the employee gets an offer of work. Once a starting date is negotiated, the new employee begins an induction process. During this practice, the employee familiarizes themselves with the organization and establishes an understanding of the expectations of the role they have been hired to do. This phase also includes the probationary period. The employee can, of course, be recruited from within or outside the business. The induction and onboarding process can vary, depending on where the recruit comes from.

During the development phase, the employee is given opportunities to gain experience and develop, both personally and functionally. As I mentioned earlier, most of these training opportunities are based on building ability to do their current and future jobs better. The training and development practice is not a one-off arrangement. This practice continues for most of the employee's time in the job. It should also be pointed out that training and development covers a wide range of learning experiences, some formal, in a classroom and others, informal or experiential. Generally, the training and development plan is preceded by a training needs analysis to determine the needs and priorities of the organization and the employees.

The other developing practice in the framework is the practice of *functioning and contributing*. This practice involves the way the jobholder interacts with the job and work needed. This includes a wide range of activity from coaching, job design and engagement, teamwork, and the like. I will primarily focus on job design and the relationship between the jobholder and the job needed. I believe this is a source for growth and one that HR can drive for greater levels of engagement and meaning. In other words, it involves clarifying their role and the way the jobholder can contribute to business success. This centers on their job description and the communication with their colleagues and supervisor.

Next is the rewarding phase. This phase covers three practices: *renumerating and rewarding*, *promoting and succession*, and *appraising and reviewing*. We'll spend a fair bit of time here. This includes payment decisions and extrinsic rewards, promotion, and succession planning, and appraising and reviewing performance. Ultimately, this phase can be summarized as the means of reinforcing to the employee the positive behaviors that contribute to organizational and individual performance.

And finally, we have the resigning and exiting phase. This is the phase where the employee decides to move to new opportunities, either through self-employment or employed in another organization. Since people are spending less and less time employed in the one company, this phase is becoming increasingly prominent in an employee's life, as is the first phase of starting. For some time now, businesses have been grappling with this higher turnover of staff. Issues of attraction and retention of star performers is an area that has occupied the attention of HR for several decades, and will, undoubtedly, continue.

This employee lifecycle framework doesn't account for periods of self-employment. The focus is on employment in an organizational setting. But a stage of self-employment seems increasingly likely in the career of an employee in the future. The benefits of self-employment are clear—work flexibility, not having to answer to a boss, getting to choose the work you want to do, and more.

Unsurprisingly, there's a huge gap in the United States between the percentage of Americans who are self-employed and the percentage of Americans who want to be self-employed (Miller 2021).[5] In the Bureau of Labor Statistics July 2010 report, roughly 10 million out of 140 million, or 7 percent of full-time working Americans are self-employed. Full-time, in this report, refers to those working over 34 hours a week. These data points show a 10:1 ratio of Americans who want to be self-employed versus those who are. That's a stark difference.

And it makes me really interested to find out what these people's reasons are for wishing to make the leap to self-employment. The self-employment choice may be a survival strategy for those who cannot find any other means of earning an income. Or it could be evidence of enterprising spirit and a desire to be one's own boss. Either way, with the accessibility and increasing sophistication of technology, it's likely to be an easier transition to self-employment now than before. Does this mean that more people will take the choice to be self-employed in the future? It may be. But we'll focus attention on those employees when they are working in organizational settings, where HR has a direct impact.

Next, we'll look more closely at these HR practices and define them in general terms.

Ten Key Takeaways

1. The employee lifecycle framework supplies a foundation to explore the issues raised in the book.
2. An employee is not an asset. It's what the employee can possibly offer that's the asset.
3. HR's primary role is to provide a conducive working environment for employees to flourish.
4. The four phases an employee goes through during their employment in any organization are starting, developing, rewarding, and parting.
5. The employee journey begins at the recruitment stage.
6. During the development phase, the employee is given opportunities to gain experience and develop, both personally and functionally.
7. Next is the rewarding phase covering renumerating and rewarding, promoting and succession, and appraising and reviewing.
8. And finally, we have the resigning and exiting phase.
9. This employee lifecycle framework doesn't account for periods of self-employment.
10. The self-employment option may be a survival strategy for those who cannot find any other means of earning an income. Or it could be evidence of entrepreneurial spirit and a desire to be one's own boss.

CHAPTER 5

The Big HR Mindset Shifts

The central question for HR is: How can the organization design the workplace to inspire the best from its employees?

Organizations are increasingly investing in the employee experience—and for good reason. A positive employee experience improves the customer experience, supports attraction and retention, increases trust in the firm and drives productivity. (Mercer 2019)[1]

In the previous chapter, I discussed the concept of the employee lifecycle. The employee lifecycle consists of four phases an employee goes through when employed in the one organization. Within each phase there are several HR practices. The way each practice is managed is based on certain beliefs. These principles drive HR behavior.

In this chapter, I introduce the 13 mindsets that need changing. I present a second model juxtaposing the traditional and new mindsets and briefly outline these shifts. This chapter concludes PART 1. We subsequently explore each mindset in some detail in PARTS 2, 3, 4, and 5. Each of these sections concentrates on one of the four phases of the employee lifecycle.

The following Table 5.1 illustrates the mindset shifts that will guide and inform the discussions for the rest of the book.

As you see, the four phases in the employee lifecycle are in the left-hand column. In the second column are 13 traditional mindsets that have guided HR practices for decades. The third column illustrates the 13 corresponding mindset shifts necessary now and in the future. I will give a brief introduction to each of these 13 mindset shifts in the remainder of the chapter.

I acknowledge that many companies are in transit between the current and new thinking. It's undoubtedly true too that a small number

Table 5.1 HR mindset shifts

| Phases | Mindset shifts | |
	Current	Future
Starting	Shift 1—past behavior Shift 2—onboarding Shift 3—onsite Shift 4—them and us	future potential integration hybrid working collaboration
Developing	Shift 5—training Shift 6—job Shift 7—job description Shift 8—job design Shift 9—competition	multidimensional learning nonjob roles role description job redesign partnership
Rewarding	Shift 10—technical knowhow Shift 11—appraising Shift 12—carrot and stick	people leadership developing performance human spirit and work
Parting	Shift 13—exit interviews	building networks

of businesses have made a successful shift to the future states illustrated in the third column. I also observe that there are many companies who are stuck in the old thinking reflected in the second column. The third perspective is that many companies are a mix of current and future states.

For example, they may have abolished their traditional appraisal system and moved to a process of regular developmental conversations between managers and team members (Shift 11). But that same company may still be wedded to selecting new hires solely based on their past experience and not developed a process to assess future potential (Shift 1). Regardless of where your organization may sit, the model gives you a useful tool to evaluate your HR practices in the context of the employee lifecycle.

The other point I want to make before summarizing each shift is this: Shifts 3 and 4 have been included in the starting phase of the employee lifecycle. They may seem out of place in the model and don't relate directly to the starting phase. However, I believe the issues of where one works (remotely or in the office) and the employment relationship are important factors in the employee's work experience. So, I included shifts 3 and 4 in the starting phase for that reason.

Let's now briefly define each of the 13 mindset shifts. I have devoted one chapter to each of these mindset shifts. I want to address two important questions in these chapters:

- Why should HR embrace the new mindset?
- What are some of the considerations necessary for HR to make the shift?

Should you wish to read forward and consider any of these 13 mindset shifts in more detail, I've identified the relevant chapter at the end of each description for convenience.

Where the Rubber Meets the Road

Failures Are Your Friend

The surest sign of a toxic culture is one in which employees never fail. The reason: a lack of failure means your employees are too afraid to take the risks that are necessary for your organization to grow.

Failure isn't just tolerated at *Scopely*, it's celebrated.

At the end of each week, the company holds a "Fail of the Week" session, during which a member of each team shares their most epic failure and what he or she learns from it.

The point isn't to call out people's mistakes but to acknowledge failure's critical role in the growth process, as well as share the lessons learned from the experience (Murphy 2021).[2]

Shifts 1 and 2 are related directly to the starting phase of the employee's lifecycle. Shifts 3 and 4, as I said earlier, are indirectly related to a starting employee.

Shift 1—Past Behavior to Future Potential

During the starting phase in the employee lifecycle, the successful job applicant is likely to have demonstrated to the selection panel that their experience and background is the best match for the job. Behavioral interviewing techniques assume that past behavior is the best predictor of future performance. While experience is still important and relevant, the emphasis needs to shift to future potential.

This shift in thinking is relevant to other HR practices besides recruitment and selection. Instead of assuming that behavior is fixed, assessing potential, and building upon the strengths and innate talents of people is more pertinent for the changing organization. For instance, the work in a firm is likely to change more rapidly. And therefore, by assessing potential, it will be a better predictor of future success.

This idea is developed in Chapter 6.

Shift 2—Onboarding to Integration

Once the employee has been selected, signed a contract, and negotiated a commencement date, they are subjected to induction training. Most firms these days do a reasonably good job inducting new employees into the business.

Induction training is familiarizing the new employee with how things operate, who they need to discuss business with, and important protocols and procedures. The onboarding process usually lasts a little longer. Onboarding ensure that the new hire understands the values and culture of the organization.

Traditional induction and onboarding have one thing in common— they both focus on helping the new employee to fit into their new workplace. It's a one-way process. It's all about the organization. Although this is still important, we need another step: integration. Integration is the idea that the company should better understand the new employee and how their strengths can be utilized to change the organization. A process of integration answers questions such as: How can the organization change to accommodate the assets a new employee brings to the new workplace? What can the business do to better harness the strengths and innate talents of the recruit? Integration brings some balance to the induction and onboarding process.

This idea is discussed in Chapter 7.

Shift 3—Onsite to Hybrid Working

Although this shift affects employees throughout their working life, as I mentioned earlier, I've addressed this in the starting phase of the employee lifecycle.

Working remotely in some shape or form is here to stay. It's a reality that needs to be embraced. Accepting this reality requires some more careful consideration around some of the challenge's organizations face when working with employees remotely. The movement toward remote working has been gaining momentum over the past decade. However, the pandemic has accelerated this trend to a point where we need to adopt a hybrid working arrangement mentality.

I address some of the challenges to make a hybrid working model functional in Chapter 8.

Shift 4—Them and Us to Collaboration

Although creating a productive workplace culture is within the domain of HR, I argue that the foundation of culture is the type of employment relationship in the workplace. HR can (and should) lead the way in promoting the evolution of a new employment relationship between managers and employees. The old *them and us* employment relationship or traditional psychological contract seems at first glance to be an artifact of the twentieth century. However, it's still alive.

Some managers see their role as directing their workforce and some employees want excessive direction from their boss. What can HR do to cultivate a new employment compact, one based on collaboration rather than a clear delineation of roles and responsibilities?

We address this mindset shift in Chapter 9.

Shifts 5 to 9 are related to the development phase of the employee lifecycle.

Shift 5—Training to Multidimensional Learning

As part of the employee's development, they are given training opportunities sponsored by their employer. Most of these training opportunities assist the employee to become more effective at their current and future job within the company. What's more, many of these training opportunities are done formally in groups either in a room or virtually. There's a place for formal training now and in the future.

But training needs to be balanced with other L&D opportunities. A multidimensional approach to L&D covers four dimensions: job-centered, person-centered, problem-centered, and machine-centered. Applying this multidimensional L&D model is an eclectic approach that better equips the employee to function effectively in a VUCA world.

I address this in Chapter 10 in PART 3.

Shift 6—Job to Nonjob Roles

Industry's overreliance on the job description means that nonjob roles are neglected. Many nonjob roles are becoming even more critical to work performance. Owing to the dependence on the job description and the downplaying of nonjob roles, employees can be forgiven for thinking that nonjob roles don't count in work performance. This disparity needs readdressing.

The concept of nonjob roles isn't new. But our fixation on the job description means that we pay very little attention to nonjob roles until they are violated.

We consider four vital nonjob roles in Chapter 11 and how they need elevating in the consciousness of managers and employees.

Shift 7—Job Description to Role Description

The job description has outlived its purpose. Its focus is on the technical requirements of the job. This can lead to a situation where the jobholder can complete the literal requirements of the job description and underperform. As I explained earlier, it's nonjob roles that are often neglected because of the importance we place on the job's KPIs. Jobs are evolving, and the job description is increasingly inadequate at identifying what people should do at work.

Instead of a job description, we need to move toward role descriptions. The role description as I explain it encompass both job and nonjob roles. This is a more appropriate work document for the modern workplace.

I explain how this can be achieved in Chapter 12.

Shift 8—Job Design to Job Redesign

Job specification is the job design method that's been in existence since the Henry Ford assembly line. This job design method has served business well. But it's too restrictive now to promote creative thinking. In the dynamic marketplace, job specification stifles independent judgment, flexibility, and agility. It constrains the employee from thinking laterally.

We need a mechanism for job redesign. This can be done by personalizing jobs using job crafting. Job crafting can loosen the rigidity of job specification. Job specification and job crafting can be combined for job redesign.

We covered job redesign concept in Chapter 13.

Shift 9—Competition to Partnership

People are fearful that AI will take their job. For decades we have viewed technology as a threat to human jobs. AI has been thought of as competition in the job market. As more and more technology is introduced to make businesses more profitable, this threat is heightened. Many employees see themselves in competition with machines for jobs.

But we need to change our perspective about AI. A more constructive mindset is one that views humans and machines working in partnership. After all, AI isn't going away and nor are employees, at least in the short-to-medium term. We need to work in a true partnership with technology in what has recently been conceptualized as super teams.

I explain what super teams are and the paradigm shift from competition to partnership in Chapter 14.

Shifts 10 to 12 are associated with the rewarding phase of the employee lifecycle.

Shift 10—Technical Knowhow to People Leadership

When we promote people into leadership roles, why is it that we still base this on their technical capabilities? We do know, for instance, that the best engineer doesn't necessarily make the best leader of engineers. Instead of relying on technical knowhow when promoting people into leadership roles, a better approach is to look for leadership attributes.

Succession planning and talent development should work in tandem. The ideas of succession planning and internal mobility to fill gaps now and in the future are not going away. But the way we do this must change. Specifically, how we assess and develop candidates for internal promotion needs a rethink. This also includes external hires too. Technical skills and knowledge are, and always will be, valuable. But leadership needs more than this and means that talent development programs can be improved to find future potential leaders.

We discussed this issue in Chapter 15.

Shift 11—Appraising to Developing Performance

If we are taking part in an ever-changing marketplace, then performance development is more useful than performance management. Ongoing development rather than one-off appraisals can only be effective with a more collaborative working relationship between managers and employees. Instead of being the boss, managers would be better served being partners in employee development. To help performance development, managers ought to apply the skills of coaching. This requires a different type of dialog between manager and employee.

Despite this, some aren't ready to give up their performance review. I authored the popular book, *The End of the Performance Review: A New Approach to Appraising Employee Performance*[3] in 2013. Even though it was written eight years ago, it has been a painfully slow evolution to developmental conversations between managers and employees. The performance review, occurring once or twice a year, in a VUCA world is pointless, a waste of time and money, and symptomatic of outdated thinking.

I refer to this shift in Chapter 16.

Shift 12—Carrot and Stick to Human Spirit and Work

In the rewarding phase of the employee lifecycle, for too long we have used carrots and sticks to motivate people at work. Authors such as Daniel Pink his book, *Drive: The Surprising Truth About Motivation*[4] claim that the carrot and stick approach isn't particularly effective and can be detrimental for boosting knowledge workers' motivation levels. How do we create an environment where people bring their hearts and minds to work with them? If the high levels of employee disengagement are an indicator, we have failed. How is intrinsic motivation fostered in the people that work in organizations?

I consider some ways to do this and to shift the reward regime from extrinsic to intrinsic motivation.

We look at the need to engage hearts and minds instead of using carrots and sticks in Chapter 17.

The final shift is related to the parting phase of employment.

Shift 13—Exit Interviews to Building Networks

We need a paradigm shift from leaving to staying connected. The last thing an employee usually does—after the farewell morning tea—is have an exit interview with HR. This interview is to benefit the organization. *Now that you are leaving, tell me frankly why.* HR is hoping from these last exchanges that they can learn future lessons. These exit interviews assume that this is the last time we will see or hear from the exiting employee.

But this is neither helpful nor realistic, particularly if the employee has been an asset to the organization through the work they've done. More and more large companies are implementing alumni programs to stay in touch with their past employees. This serves a host of benefits, including the possibility that employee may be valuable for short-term assignments or be rehired in the future.

I discuss shifting from leaving to staying connected in Chapter 18.

The one common theme in all these 13 mindset shifts is the employee. I'm suggesting that by focusing on the employee lifecycle, HR can become employee centric in its intent and approach. After all, shouldn't the employee be the center of the work that HR does? It's probably no different than an architect concentrating their energies on designing great buildings.

If we accept that employee potential is a business's greatest asset, as I suggest in Chapter 3, then everything that is said, done, and thought about should have the employee top-of-mind. The central question for HR is: How can the organization design the workplace to inspire the best from its employees? HR is key for individual and organization success and will continue to be for some time. But to achieve this, HR must create an environment (and remove barriers) for people to bring their whole self to work. This is the main theme of the book.

In PART 2, we look at the starting phase of the employee lifecycle.

Ten Key Takeaways

1. This chapter covers the HR mindset shifts model.
2. The 13 mindset shifts relate to the four phases of the employee lifecycle framework.
3. Future potential, integration, hybrid working, and collaboration are the future mindset shifts for the starting phase of the employee lifecycle.
4. Multidimensional learning, nonjob roles, role descriptions, job redesign, and partnership are the five mindset shifts in the developing phase of the employee lifecycle.
5. People leadership, developing performance, and human spirit and work are the three new mindsets for the rewarding phase of the employee lifecycle.
6. Building networks is the new mindset shift for the parting phase of the employee life cycle.
7. It's acknowledged that many companies are in transit between the current and new thinking.
8. Two questions are addressed about each of these mindset shifts: Why should HR embrace the new mindset? And what are some of the considerations necessary for HR to make the shift?

9. One common theme in all 13 mindset shifts is the employee.

10. If we accept that employee potential is a business's greatest asset, then everything that is said, done, and thought about should have the employee top of mind.

PART 2

Starting Phase
of Employment

CHAPTER 6

Shift 1: Past Performance to Future Potential

Instead of looking for a person suited to a specific job criterion, ironically, we should be looking for a person suited to flexibly deploying their skills in a wide range of work contexts.

The rise of general manager Phil Nolan to the executive ranks of his company, a market leader in laundry products, was due in large part to his role-model qualities. Phil was placed in charge of the firm's troubled core product, a liquid detergent whose sales were in a multiyear downward slide. Two high-visibility marketing managers had each been given a chance to reinvigorate product sales. Both had tried price-reduction tactics, to no avail. Then it was Phil's turn. But, with a background in product development rather than marketing, he was the dark horse candidate.

Fortunately, corporate executives saw more in Phil, who had engineered a turnaround at a troubled product-development group by fostering cooperative relationships and teamwork. Highly trustworthy, he could engage people in very candid conversations about business challenges. As a result, he was able to get to the core of a problem quickly and find workable solutions. Phil not only was superb at motivating people, but also had a keen eye for patterns and an impressive strategic vision. He applied all those skills to the new assignment.

Within the first year in his new role, Phil led his team to grow product sales by 30%. In our interview with the company's HR executive, the interviewee emphasized Phil's ability to win people over: "There is humility to him despite the fact that he is now the public face of the brand. Phil helps his peers succeed rather than threatening them. He is a role model for the organization." (Ready, Conger, and Hill 2010)[1]

In PART 2, we consider the mindset shifts associated with the starting phase of employment. We begin with recruitment and selection.

When one casts their eyes around the people they work with, it's not hard to identify people with potential. We are familiar with the traits of the people we work closely with. Although hiring someone from outside the company and assessing their potential is more challenging. Assessing candidate's potential, regardless of whether they're within or outside the firm, is increasingly more important in a dynamic workplace. In a changing work setting, future potential is more valuable than past experience. I'm not suggesting that experience doesn't count. It does. It always will. But it's only one ingredient in the successful hiring recipe.

With the world transforming at a dizzying rate, beyond apparent major trends, it's tricky to predict what the future holds. What's worked in the past is therefore no guarantee that it will work in the future. With the relentless intrusion of AI, the way jobs are done is constantly transforming. Some jobs are disappearing. Some jobs are emerging. In this milieu, future potential rather than past competency is more prized.

Although we can't predict the future with certainty, we can define the attributes necessary to adapt to an ever-changing environment. What's more, we can identify and measure these traits in job candidates. Unsurprisingly, there is a proliferation of tools to assess a person's potential. These diagnostic tools will undoubtedly become more sophisticated and accurate.

What Is Future Potential?

Potential in this context is how quickly and effectively a person can adapt and respond to changes in their surrounding work environment. Douglas Ready and colleagues in their Harvard Business Review article, *Are You a High Potential?* define high potentials as,

> ... consistently and significantly outperforming their peer groups in a variety of settings and circumstances. While achieving these superior levels of performance, they exhibit behaviors that reflect their companies' culture and values in an exemplary manner. Moreover, they show a strong capacity to grow and succeed

throughout their careers within an organization—more quickly and effectively than their peer groups do. (Ready, Conger, and Hill 2010)[2]

They identify four traits they call X factors:

- Drive to excel
- Catalytic learning capability
- Enterprising spirit
- Dynamic sensors.[3]

As I said, it's easy to observe these traits in the workplace. But it becomes more challenging to assess these attributes in the recruitment and selection process, particularly for "outsiders." There are several profiling instruments that can do this reasonably accurately. For example, the *High Potential Trait Indicator* (HPTI) was developed by Ian McRae and Adrian Furnham in 2006.[4] The HPTI was designed using an "optimality" model, which assumes that certain personality traits are considered "optimal" requirements for certain jobs.

This tool measures *conscientiousness*, *adjustment*, *curiosity*, *risk approach*, *ambiguity*, *acceptance*, and *competitiveness*. HPTI assesses each trait against a job role. Too much or too little of a trait can have advantages as well as disadvantages in certain work contexts. Trait levels are determined as predictive indicators of high potential for success. Depending on the work, some indicators highlight characteristics that may adversely affect the success of an otherwise high potential employee.

The time-honored hiring practice is based on evidence of traditional competencies and previous work experience. This process involves matching square pegs for square holes and round pegs for round holes. The assumption is to find the best match between the job applicant and the vacant position.

The work of an organization is broken down into many series of tasks and activities. An analysis groups similar tasks and activities into a job specification. A job specification is a detailed description of a job role, including all its responsibilities, goals, and requirements. The job description contextualizes the job specification. It includes a job title, work location, job summary, working environment, duties to be performed, and how they'll be measured. I have more to say about the job specification and its bed fellow, the job description in Chapters 12 and 13.

These documents supply the yardstick to assess the qualifications, competences, and experience of a candidate applying to fill a job. The applicant with the best match usually gets hired. But this model's sustainability must be questioned for two reasons. First, the volatility of the marketplace and a company's response makes a job specification redundant quickly. Second, the battle to keep and attract top talent is fierce. Companies need to find and keep people with high potential to gain a competitive edge. High potential traits aren't usually part of a job specification. These two drivers diminish the value of job specification.

Jobs and the work they encapsulate change rapidly. And this means that the way we design jobs is outmoded. So, applying the competency-based model to select new hires is deficient. Instead of looking for a person suited to a specific job criterion, ironically, we should be looking for a person suited to flexibly deploying their skills in a wide range of work contexts. In Chapter 9, *flexible deployment* is one of eight shared beliefs to replace *specialized employment* of a new employment relationship. The idea of matching people to a job specification is no longer viable.

What's the Solution?

In place of focusing exclusively on a job's specified competencies, we need to also account for future potential. An astute hire today is someone capable of retrofitting their capabilities to the ever-changing business milieu and be able to grow into challenging emerging roles.

According to Claudio Fernández-Aráoz, in his article, *21st-Century Talent Spotting*, companies must assess current and prospective employees on five key success indicators:

- The right motivation
- Curiosity
- Insight
- Engagement
- Determination[5]

The *right motivation* is defined as a burning desire to excel, while working collaboratively with colleagues. People with potential usually have above average aspirations and want to leave their mark on the work they do. They have a mindset of continuous personal improvement; always trying to better themselves. Fernández-Aráoz makes an important distinction between individual and collective motivation.

The right motivation isn't a selfish aspiration. People with high potential are willing and able to work with and through other people to get the job done. Being a team player is a critical attribute of high potential. I discuss this nonjob role in Chapter 11. Single-minded motivation is not the right motivation in the workplace.

Curiosity is proactively exploring new ideas and experiences. People with curiosity are likely to invite and accept feedback, even if it's not complimentary. A high potential is always looking for improvement in themselves and the way they do things. To do this, they're open to learning and change.

Insight is the ability to gather necessary information and be able to make sense of it. This understanding can then be applied by considering new possibilities to solve old problems. They are willing, in other words, to look at problems from different perspectives and come up with new angles. *If it ain't broke don't fix it,* is not part of their language.

Engagement is the capacity to inspire and influence others. You don't need to be a manager to motivate and persuade colleagues. Engagement is the ability to see the big picture and take others on that journey, regardless of one's position in the organizational pecking order.

And *determination*, is characterized by the tenacity to stick to a problem regardless of how difficult it is, until a solution is found. People with determination can bounce back from adversity.

These characteristics, I'm sure you'd agree, summarize potential. Not all current and potential employees possess these qualities. Only a small percentage are likely to exhibit these traits. Nonetheless, if the selection panel by-passes these attributes—with a mission to find the "best" fit for a job vacancy—then the firm is missing an opportunity to hire based on potential. These traits (or lack of them) become apparent once a new employee commences work. But we must make them an integral part of the selection process.

These indicators of high potential are measurable, or at least discoverable, by asking carefully crafted questions at the interview. If you look closely at Fernández-Aráoz's five success factors, they have one common denominator—they're indicators of a person's ability to learn new, and unlearn, outdated skills. If someone has this ability to learn and unlearn, they can transition into new roles relatively easier than someone without these traits.

According to Fernández-Aráoz,

Potential is the most important predictor of success at all levels, from junior management to the C-Suite and the board … I'm convinced that organizations and their leaders must transition to what I think of as a new era of talent spotting—one in which their evaluations of one another are based not on brawn, brains, experience, or competencies, but on potential. (Fernández-Aráoz 2014)[6]

Competency-based appraisals and appointments are undoubtedly becoming increasingly insufficient to cater for the needs of a dynamic business. We need to accept the reality that when the competitive environment changes, what makes someone successful today, might not be a success tomorrow.

The changing world of work involves more than the way tasks and activities are done, or not done. It also means leading and collaborating with different groups of colleagues. The fluid nature of interpersonal interactions and the ability to work effectively with a wide range of people needs consideration in this selection process. Having the right skill set is still important. But being able to collaborate with others in a spirit of continuous improvement is crucial too.

By adjusting the selection criteria to accommodate these changes, hiring for potential can be accomplished. Behavioral-based interviewing has been the popular way to assess candidates at the interview. This popular interviewing technique strives to discover how the interviewee acted in previous employment-related situations. The logic supporting this approach is how one behaved in the past is a predictor of how they are likely to act in the future. Past behavior predicts future performance, in other words. The problem here isn't the technique; rather, it is how it's used.

Behavioral-based selection interviewing still has its place. But why limit its use to questions about competencies in the job specification? Why not broaden the scope to include questions around the high potential attributes we've just discussed? I think the selection process needs a better balance between job competencies and personal traits.

You may be thinking: I understand the value of these attributes of potential, but how can they be gauged? The answer: In the same way, we assess applicant's job competencies. Explore the candidate's personal and professional history. Ask good questions to review these traits. Follow-up the candidate's referees with similar questions around potential.

To gauge an applicant's motivation, for instance, you need to do more than ask what drives them. Instead, look for past critical incidents, if they exist, that illustrate the candidate's personal tenacity and commitment while working collaboratively. Asking open-ended questions that focus on their experiences in delivering results under trying circumstances. Are there occasions when they worked cooperatively with other people they didn't know? How did they do that? Here is such a question: *Describe a situation where you were facing a complex problem in your previous work and how you went about resolving this?* In the same way, you look for illustrations of one's job competences, ask for instances where the right motivation has been demonstrated in the past. These examples can be validated with thorough reference checking.

Where the Rubber Meets the Road

Stretch Development

Jonathan Harvey, a top HR executive at ANZ, an Australian bank that operates in 33 countries, has this to say about high potentials:
"When it comes to developing executives for future leadership assignments, we are constantly striving to find the optimal level of discomfort in the next role or project, because that's where the most learning happens. We don't want people to be stretched beyond their limits. But we want well rounded, values-focused leaders who see the world through a wide-angle lens, and the right stretch assignments are what helps people get there."[7]

The bottom line: Jobs are changing so rapidly that we can't predict the competences needed to succeed in the future, even in a few years' time. So, the focus on hiring needs to shift from a predominantly competency-based selection approach to a balanced approach that considers potential. This doesn't mean neglecting technical experience and competency. But it does mean gauging with more rigor nonjob attributes besides job experience, competences, and qualifications. We can't rely totally on job traits when making hiring decisions. It makes sense to add another layer of criteria that focuses on the potential of applicants to be flexible and maneuverable in our rapidly changing world.

In the next chapter, I want to explore the next practice the successful hire faces in their employment journey: induction and onboarding.

Ten Key Takeaways

1. Assessing candidate's potential, regardless of whether they're within or outside the firm, is increasingly more important in a dynamic workplace.
2. What's worked in the past is therefore no guarantee that it will work in the future.
3. Although we can't predict the future with certainty, we can define the attributes necessary to adapt to an ever-changing environment.
4. Potential is how quickly and effectively a person can adapt and respond to changes in their surrounding work environment.
5. Jobs and the work they encapsulate change rapidly. And this means that the way we design jobs is outmoded.
6. In place of focusing exclusively on a job's specified competencies, we need to also account for future potential.
7. Five key success indicators of potential are: the right motivation, curiosity, insight, engagement, and determination.
8. Only a small percentage are likely to exhibit these traits.
9. These indicators of high potential are measurable, or at least discoverable, by asking carefully crafted questions at the interview.
10. We can't rely totally on job traits when making hiring decisions.

CHAPTER 7

Shift 2: Induction to Integration

At many organizations, onboarding processes have a common theme: indoctrinating new employees into the organizational culture.

> The first day of a new employee is commonly structured around introducing them to the work environment and company culture. In addition to the plethora of forms new employees are asked to fill out, they hear about why the organization they have joined is so special. They learn about the company's founders, its values and why they should be proud to be a part of the organization. The overriding goal is to show new employees "how things are done around here" and to instill in them a sense of pride in their new affiliation. At many organizations, onboarding processes have a common theme: indoctrinating new employees into the organizational culture. (Cable, Gino, and Staats 2013)[1]

Once the employee is selected, agrees to accept the offer, and negotiates a starting time to commence their new job, they're subjected to what has commonly referred to as induction training. The induction and onboarding process has improved significantly in the last 30 years. But I think it's time to revisit this practice.

A One-Way Street

My main concern is that it's a one-way street. The employee is thoroughly introduced to the organization, but not the other way round. Induction and onboarding are all about the newbie being molded and shaped to fit into the organizational structure. This is a process of indoctrination rather than integration. The recruit's manager is usually inviting and spends time find out a little about them. But that's the extent of it. It's now a two-way process. It's about the new employee being accommodating to suit the needs and interests of their new employer. It's rarely about the company adapting to harness the strengths of the individual.

I'm not suggesting throwing out the induction program. But it can be improved with another stage of integration to complement induction and onboarding.

The company in the early stage of the employee lifecycle typically does a reasonable job at socializing them into the ways of the business. There's no real inclination for the business to adjust to the starting employee's strengths, preferences, or interests. This may come later, if at all. The question: *How can the company benefit from what the starting employee has to offer, apart from filling a vacancy?* isn't asked. Yet, there's undoubtedly assets a new hire can offer that go untapped. For example, the recruit may have a gift at dealing with customers beyond the technical role they're hired to do. Or, they may have certain knowledge of the marketplace the business is operating in that's gold and goes unrecognized. With more effort to make the induction process two-way, these assets are unearthed. Keen to make a good first impression, in the traditional induction program, the new employee may feel disinclined to mention these strengths, feeling a certain pressure to fall into line.

Induction and onboarding are vital for several reasons. We know statistically that the most vulnerable time in the employee lifecycle is doing this early stage of employment. Employees are more likely to leave during this phase than at any other stage in their employment. These statistics shouldn't be ignored. They suggest the process could be improved. What's more, it's very costly to replace an employee. Most of the calculated costs of replacing an employee don't consider "job lag."

Job Lag

Job lag is a reasonably new term (Baker 2014).[2] The real cost of replacing an employee is best explained by job lag. I define it as the total cost of suboptimal performance during the full duration of employee turnover. Suboptimal performance starts from the time an employee voluntarily or involuntarily gives or receives notice of their termination. And job lag continues up to the time the replacement employee reaches optimal productivity. This cost of job lag is a significant hidden cost to business.

Optimal performance is defined as the point when an employee is fully contributing to the level of output expected of an established worker in that role. This cost isn't factored into most calculations of the financial burden of employee turnover.

Most of the writing on the indirect costs of employee turnover doesn't consider the inevitable decline in an employee's productivity once they've decided to leave. This decline can start before they give formal notice. Since the exiting employee's focus is elsewhere, it's likely they aren't fully engaged in their current work. And when their replacement starts, it's likely that it will take several months in their new job to reach optimal performance, even with relevant experience. The replacement needs time to familiarize themselves with the new job.

The suboptimal productivity of the exiting and replacement employee combines to calculate the costs of job lag. This cost can then be added to the direct costs of recruiting and selecting a replacement.

Briefly, an equation for calculating the factors involved in job lag can be summed up this way: The period from notice of termination to actual termination + the time it takes to replace the terminated employee + the origins of the replacement employee + the time it takes for the new employee to reach optimal productivity = job lag. This equation doesn't account for the other costs in the recruitment and selection process, such as advertising.

I have estimated the annual financial burden on organizations and the economy, in general, in Australia to be at least $6.5 billion per annum (Baker 2014).[3] It would inevitably be higher in the United States and other larger countries.

In financial terms, the costs of suboptimal performance are two-fold. First, the company needs to absorb the cost of paying wages to an employee who is working below the expected level of performance. This includes the exiting and starting employee. Second, the added costs associated with suboptimal performance are related to the costs to business revenue. Whether an employee collaborates directly with customers (such as a salesperson) or indirectly in an internal service role, such as HR, business income will be adversely affected with a drop in their performance. While job lag is to some extent unavoidable, it can be managed.

Job lag costs can be minimized substantially by addressing factors related to this inevitable period of reduced productivity. The obvious answer to minimizing the fiscal impact of job lag is reducing employee turnover. Some turnover is unavoidable—it's even healthy for a business. Turnover varies from industry to industry. But keeping and developing employees is a priority in most businesses. Employee turnover is highest, as I mentioned, within the first 90 days of employment. One report suggests that 43 percent of new employees quit in the first 90 days (Work Institute 2019).[4]

There are several factors that create job lag:

- Reasons for termination of the earlier employee.
- The industry and the nature of the work.
- The background of the employee.
- Size of the organization.
- The capabilities of the individual and their aptitude to learn on-the-job.
- The level of support the new employee receives from the company.

But it's obvious that a good induction and onboarding program can make a significant difference to high turnover levels. To off-set the elevated levels of vulnerability an employee feels during the first few weeks of a new job, a superior induction process is critical. Poor induction procedures increase the risk of turnover.

Where the Rubber Meets the Road

The Problem With Inductions

Many HR professionals believe that building and retaining talent starts on "day one" by stressing to the new employee the importance of understanding and committing to the company's values. This is the norm for many companies. It seems logical to enable newcomers to fit in quickly and conform to the business's way of doing things. At the same time, it gives leaders some control over what they can expect from new hires.

However, Daniel Cable, a professor of organizational behavior at London Business School, believe that traditional induction and onboarding has some glaring weaknesses. The assumption of this approach is that the company's values can be taught and embraced by newcomers.

"This creates a tension: When newcomers are 'processed' to accept an organization's identity, they are expected to downplay their own identities, at least while they are at work. But subordinating one's identity and unique perspectives may not be optimal in the long run for either the organization or the individual employee because suppressing one's identity is upsetting and psychologically depleting." (Cable, Gino, and Staats 2013)[5]

What's the Difference Between Induction and Onboarding?

The solution to minimizing turnover in the early stages of employment is to make induction and onboarding more collaborative. In most cases, as we know, the traditional process is one-way. Yes, the new employee is encouraged to ask questions. But these opportunities to ask questions are done in the context of an organization-specific agenda. And the agenda is about making sure the employee is in lock step with the company's systems, processes, and culture. The overriding message is: *This is the way we do things around here.*

So how do we make the induction and onboarding process more inclusive? Before I answer this, let's understand what's already in place.

What's the difference between induction and onboarding? These terms are frequently used interchangeably, but they're different.

Induction evolved from the original term *orientation*. Basically, the induction process involves introducing the organization and the job to the new employee. It enables the new starter to become familiar with their surroundings as quickly as possible. Otherwise, without a decent induction plan, the new employee is thrown in at the deep end of the swimming pool.

Onboarding is a process that generally is delivered over several months to assist new hires to fully adjust to the social and performance aspects of their new job. New employees in the onboarding process learn the attitudes, knowledge, skills, and behaviors required to function effectively within the business. The assumption is that by making a new hire feel welcome and getting them up to speed in their new job, they'll be able to successfully contribute to business outcomes. Onboarding involves building relationships, setting expectations, improving role clarity, strengthening commitment, and developing the employee's knowledge of the prevailing culture.

As we discussed earlier, job lag is a serious cost to business. And so, if done more effectively, induction training can reduce business costs. High turnover in the early stages of employment doesn't only affect employees. It's estimated that 50 percent of managers fail within the first 18 months. Other research suggests that 50 percent of employees leave within the first four months.[6] According to the Human Capital Institute, a staggering 20 percent of new hires leave for a new opportunity within the first 45 days on the job (Human Capital Institute 2019).[7] Regardless of whether its managers or employees, it's apparent given the true costs of job turnover that the induction (and onboarding) process needs to do more to ensure that people don't leave after several weeks in a new role.

Investors in People offer accreditation to organizations that adhere to certain standards. They emphasize the need to be clear about induction and onboarding:

> Inductions have a long history, but onboarding is the new kid on the block. High-performing organizations should, of course, do both. But how do you avoid blurred lines, duplicated effort, and confusion? By understanding the differences between induction and onboarding and making sure you get both right. (Investors in People)[8]

So, let's clear up the distinction. Induction is very much about the practical and technical integration into the organization. It's where the form filling happens. Inductions help people understand the basic needs and logistics within the business. There's usually an initial glut of information. A new employee will go home after their first day with their head spinning from all the information thrown at them. There's probably a safety induction. There's a meet and greet with stakeholders and team members. Several presentations. It's a formulaic procedure. The information is highly structured and reasonably generic. Although there are opportunities to ask questions, inductions, which may extend beyond the first day, are pretty much a one-way series of monologs rather than dialogs. The induction is a necessary part of the onboarding process.

The purpose of onboarding is to familiarize the new hire with the demands and requirements of the business. During onboarding a new employee can be assigned a buddy or mentor. There's a greater emphasis on building interpersonal relationships during onboarding. This involves building trust between the individual and their immediate work colleagues and their manager. As the new employee builds relationships and trust with their new workmates, they start to learn more informal aspects of how the organization works and what's required. These colleagues, socialized the same way, explain how the employee can survive and thrive in the business. Onboarding delivers context and understanding.

Onboarding is generally done on the job. So, it has a lot to do with the work that's required, the standards expected, and a familiarization with the manager's ways. KPIs are discussed. The process, although less formal than induction, can last several weeks and months. Onboarding varies depending on the industry, size of the business, and the interpersonal dynamics. It's less one-way than the induction process. Given the employee is still finding their feet, they're often on the receiving end of well-meaning advice and instructions, however. The new employee has no real say in how things are done—they are rarely asked for their opinion.

We must also acknowledge that remote inductions and onboarding processes are more frequent, post-COVID. I discuss this in the next chapter.

Integration

Integration is an important step to add to the induction and onboarding program to assist the new person to become a fully functioning member of the team as quickly and smoothly as possible. This step isn't common practice. Egon Zehnder surveyed 588 executives at the VP level and above who had joined new companies in the past few years. Almost 60 percent reported that it took them six months—and close to 20 percent said it took more than nine months—to have a full impact in their new roles. What's more, less than a third said they had received any meaningful support during their transitions—a big problem when you consider that more than 80 percent of this minority thought such support had made a major difference in their early employment.[9] If this is the case for senior executives, then it underlines the need to make sure that a good integration process is in place for all employees.

What's missing in the current induction and onboarding process is the need for more emphasis on integration. By integration, I mean redressing the imbalance of an essentially one-sided approach in the early stages of employment. This process can be referred to as a "duolog." A duolog is a conversation between two people. It typically occurs in a play or dramatic performance in the form of a dialog limited to two speakers. It's apt for the workplace, where this is a series of conversations between the manager and the new hire, while surrounded by a hive of business activity. In the workplace, the duolog is a series of conversations between a new hire and their manager.

This duolog is a supplement to, and not a replacement for, the induction and onboarding practice. This third stage in the life of a new hire is more employee centered. Table 7.1 illustrates the proposed three-stage approach.

You'll notice that "modify the job specification" is mentioned as part of the objective for the integration stage. This concept is commonly referred to as job crafting. I discuss job crafting in detail in Chapter 13. Job crafting should start early in a new employee's lifecycle.

The idea of job crafting is to shape the work to suit the strengths and preferences of the jobholder, in this case the new employee. Instead of trying to mold the employee to fit the job specification, job crafting is a means of creating a better match between the employee and the job requirements. In the spirit of integration, job crafting attempts to answer the question: *How can the employer harness the innate talents and strengths of a new employee so that they can add more value to the business?* You might recall me talking about trying to fit a square peg in a round

Table 7.1 *Induction, onboarding, and integration*

Key concepts and stages	Induction	Onboarding	Integration
Objective	To introduce the new hire to the company's policies, practices, and procedures.	To introduce the new hire to the company's values, expectations, and working relationships.	To learn from the insights and experiences of the new hire and to modify the job specification to fully harness their strengths and interests.
Communication method	Formal one-way.	Informal one-way, with Q & A.	Informal two-way.
Focus	Company.	Business unit.	Individual.
Delivery frequency	One-off event.	Several meetings.	Fortnightly duolog.
Timeframe	Commences on first day and runs for several hours.	Three months until probation.	Ongoing.
Mode	Series of meeting.	Meetings and conversations.	One-to-one conversations between a new employee and their manager.

hole in the previous chapter. What about the idea of creating a square hole for a square peg? In other words, how can the job be better shaped to suit the jobholder? This discussion should be an integral part of the integration stage.

I'm not suggesting that the new hire has free rein; that is, they can do whatever they please. They still have specific core tasks to accomplish. However, there's always room to improve the fit between the new employee and their job. Given the cost of job lag and the importance of holding onto top talent, it makes good sense to consider job crafting as part of the integration stage.

Good managers are likely to be engaging in regular check-ins with team members. But as we know, good managers are in short supply. Therefore, duologs must be integrated into the program for new (and existing) employees. They need to be mandatory. What is discussed in these regular check-ins, apart from job crafting? I suggest using the Five Conversations Framework as a starting point. I explain this approach in PART 4 (Chapter 16).

Research consistently shows that a thorough program for new employees produce valuable outcomes, including higher job satisfaction, greater employee commitment, and better performance results. Companies who have implemented onboarding strategies, such as regular duologs, have experienced as much as a 50 percent increase in new hire retention and 54 percent greater new hire productivity (Lombardi 2011).[10] Putting the same energy into the integration stage as induction and onboarding has many benefits for the new employee and the business.

In the next chapter, I want to address some of the issues associated with remote working arrangements.

Ten Key Takeaways

1. Once the employee is selected, agrees to accept the offer, and negotiates a starting time to commence their new job, they're subjected to what has been commonly referred to as induction training.
2. The main concern is that it's a one-way street.
3. It can be improved with another stage of integration to complement induction and onboarding.
4. The real cost of replacing an employee is best explained by job lag.
5. Job lag is defined as the total cost of suboptimal performance during the full duration of employee turnover.
6. Optimal performance is defined as the point when an employee is fully contributing to the level of output expected of an established worker in that role.
7. Job lag costs can be minimized substantially by addressing factors related to this inevitable period of reduced productivity.
8. The solution to minimizing turnover in the early stages of employment is to make induction and onboarding more collaborative.
9. Integration is an important step to add to the induction and onboarding program to assist the new person to become a fully functioning member of the team as quickly and smoothly as possible.
10. Instead of trying to mold the employee to fit the job specification, job crafting is a means of creating a better match between the employee and the job requirements.

CHAPTER 8

Shift 3: Onsite to Hybrid Working

Working remotely in some form is here to stay. Most likely, work will continue in a hybrid manner.

> Kristof works directly with Sven and others, who are field staff and considered "essential workers." So, they were never sent to work remotely. Kristof, on the other hand, can work remotely most days.
>
> In July, the company's busiest month, remote workers were called back to the office. Kristof's schedule turned into a hybrid working arrangement, consisting of a few days in the office and a few days remote.
>
> On remote days, Kristof didn't have to commute, and was meeting with colleagues via zoom. He got a lot more done and was more productive with his time. On the days in the office, the technical and administrative work was slower, as he engaged with people, built relationships, and went to the field to see the physical projects he was working on.
>
> Working remotely versus working in the office meant Kristoff had to focus on various aspects of his job. Overall, as he learned to adjust, it didn't impact on his productivity or effectiveness. (Root 2021)[1]

Although the subject of remote working isn't strictly a topic for the start-up phase of employment, effective ways of conveying information to and from offsite employees is increasingly becoming an issue. More and more employees are commencing their employment remotely. This trend is likely to continue.

Businesses need to adjust to hybrid working arrangements, where employees spend part of their time working from home. Even after COVID, companies can no longer rely purely on face-to-face interactions. Without good digital solutions and communication tools, businesses will lose top talent that find hybrid working agreements appealing. Productivity will suffer if businesses are anticipating the day when everybody is working in the office. This day may never arrive again.

Working remotely in some form is here to stay. Most likely, work will continue in a hybrid manner. And irrespective of how often a person works from home, whether it's one day a week or several months, HR practices need to be fully equipped for remote work.

Are Employees More Productive Working From Home?

Many managers I spoke to during 2020 told me they were pleasantly surprised at how well many employees had adapted to working remotely. Productivity in some cases increased. What's the truth about productivity working from home?

Some research backs up these managers' claims. One of the most commonly cited studies on remote worker performance was conducted by Stanford University in 2013, well before the pandemic. The *Work from Home* (WFH) experiment was done at CTrip, a NASDAQ-listed Chinese travel company; 16,000 call center employees volunteered for the research. The nine-month study showed a 13 percent performance increase. Working more time per shift, meaning fewer breaks and less sick leave, accounted for 9 percent of the increase. Another 4 percent of productivity growth was because employees took more calls per shift. The participants reported it was easier to focus because the home environment was quieter and less distracting (Hubstaff blog 2020).[2] Productivity assessments vary depending on the industry, of course.

A more recent U.S.-based study showed a 35 percent increase in employee productivity working remotely. When Best Buy introduced a flexible work program for its employees, performance jumped dramatically. 65 percent of workers report that they felt more productive when out of the office. Of those employees who said they were more productive when working remotely, 86 percent rate their productivity as being either good or excellent (Hubstaff blog 2020).[3]

There's usually minimal organizational politics and no water cooler at home. No commute time either. I'm sure this accounts for some of this productivity boost in these studies. However, full-time remote working also has its drawbacks, with zoom fatigue quickly setting in, and extroverts itching for more social contact. Not everyone had the space to work comfortably at home. The workday extends for many as they juggled home schooling with work.

As the spread of the virus recedes and people become vaccinated, many employees are adopting a hybrid model as the best of both worlds.

There's been a lot of hype in the media about working from home and the amazing productivity gains from these new arrangements. But not all the research is positive about how productive people are working from home. We need to be mindful that these reports can be misleading. It should also be noted that productivity isn't only an organizational concern. Most employees are also interested in maintaining high levels of productivity. Productivity affects job satisfaction, not to mention job security—an important consideration at a time when people are worried about their jobs.

There's a debate currently raging on how to coax employees back into the workplace. The question being raised is: *How do we get employees back into the office?* Perhaps a better question might be: *Why they don't want to come back to the workplace?* It's likely that many employees will adopt a hybrid approach to working well after the pandemic. Of course, some jobs can't be done from home.

But as firms entertain any form of remote working activity—whether forced or voluntary—it raises lots of challenges. Face-to-face interactions, once part and parcel of work, can no longer be taken for granted.

What does it mean when research indicates that productivity improves working from home? Is it more than simply no commute time or an absence of idle chit chat? It maybe the threat people feel that spurs on more productivity. This feeling of threat is what Tracy Brower, a career consultant, calls "panic productivity."[5] Panic productivity may come from an adrenaline boost transitioning from the workplace to working remotely. In 2020, where job loss was rife, many people were undoubtedly working like crazy in the hope of staying visible, relevant, and ensuring their boss thought that they were still adding value. Brower says:

If their productivity was high at first, it has declined as the pandemic has worn on and as the stressors around them have mounted. Facilitating learning for children at home, caring for loved ones and navigating all the new norms for work are pressure points which have built over time and are unlikely to let up anytime soon.[6]

Where the Rubber Meets the Road

LondonEnergy

Jacques Samama, head of people at LondonEnergy, shares how the pandemic has affected both office-based and operational staff:

"As an operational business, we have almost 80% of our workforce who are highly operative and 20% who are office based, so remote working has always been a challenge for the whole company given most of our staff must be at work to do their job. Equally remote working has traditionally been seen by the workforce as a kind of a 'privilege' for senior managers and the leadership.

The COVID-19 period has massively changed this feeling and our practices. Firstly, we have been able to see many more employees working from home.

Despite the fact we are an operational business that works 24/7 with key worker status, more employees have been able to work remotely from home and it has proven to be very efficient.

It is also important to note that this change of culture has positively affected the perception of remote working. It is no longer seen as a privilege or an alleged way of being on weekend from Thursday afternoon, but a real 'tool' to increase efficiency at work. Some of our staff choose to work from home to focus on a particular topic where they need quietness, while some use it to ensure a decent work/life balance and so they can pick up the kids after school.

For operational staff, the main change has been about their ability to be more digital and connected on our social and communication platform.

The best example has been the implementation of a weekly call with our MD who has been able to update the company with COVID-19 news. We have now extended the agenda of this call and our MD gives everyone a weekly update on all relevant topics. In our last pulse survey,

75% of the employees recognised they have the information they need, compared to 45% six months ago.

I believe that remote working throughout this period has changed the nature of our organization by creating a more agile environment and allowed everyone from different parts of the business to remain connected which did not happen before." (Gallacher 2020)[4]

It's questionable whether productivity is sustainable (or desirable) based on threat.

Apart from productivity, there are other performance factors that should be discussed, whether working in an office or remotely. For instance, engagement, commitment, learning, creativity, and continuous improvement all contribute to performance. Productivity is one element, albeit an important one, in the overall assessment of performance.

Productivity is normally measured by how much one gets done in a set period. This measurement may be misleading in remote working environments. There's plenty of anecdotal evidence that employees work longer hours at home. People can work longer hours and produce more. Does this mean their productivity has improved? Office work is far more structured. Time limits are imposed. Expectations are easier to enforce. Down time and work time are clearly delineated. People can find it harder to switch off working from home.

We also need to account for the type of work people are doing. A recent study indicated that people working at home would be more productive on rote, routine, or repetitive tasks. In practice, this suggests that administrative responsibilities are probably easier to accomplish at home. The study also indicated that employees are less productive at home on work that is complex, urgent, or required problem solving (Künn, Seel, and Zegners 2020).[7] Work that's more multifaceted may be easier to accomplish in the office. Complex problem solving usually involves engaging with others, whereas routine work can be done solo.

Communicating with people working at a distance is undoubtedly more challenging. Even with video conferencing technology available, conversing can be problematic. In the office, you can stroll down the corridor to ask a question or seek clarification. Although many still choose to send an e-mail! But people you need to talk to in an office are often in your line-of-sight. While many tasks at work can be done individually, lots are accomplished collaboratively. These cooperative tasks often require inputs from a range of different stakeholders who are sometimes more easily accessible onsite.

So, making the claim productivity is up or down working remote is too simplistic. Nevertheless, remote working arrangements are likely to stay in some form. We need to carefully consider the challenges and implications. The pandemic has accelerated this trend toward remote working. It's also given us the opportunity to consider remote working more seriously.

Pre-COVID, remote working arrangements were becoming more and more acceptable. Some research suggests that up to 60 percent of employees were working remotely in some form and 30 percent were fully remote before the pandemic (Global Workplace Analytics 2019).[8] As we know, the crisis has pushed these numbers even higher. Many employees—not all—hope to keep working from home in the new normal. We can assume that the remote working trend will continue.

What Are the Challenges?

Although no one has all the answers, traditional management practices need to change faster to accommodate this shift. I consider the employment relationship in the next chapter. Remote working leads to greater disconnection, potentially more inefficiencies, and can have adverse effects on the business itself. This means the manager–employee relationship must adjust.

Since we're discussing the starting phase of the employee lifecycle, let's begin with the issues of interviewing, hiring, and onboarding remote workers.

Even with face-to-face interviews, the selection process can be fraught. The process is potentially more difficult finding, interviewing, and hiring candidates from a distance. Although video conferencing works extremely well, many managers still feel comfortable meeting candidates face-to-face. This provides them with the opportunity to observe important nonverbal cues.

Perhaps a more difficult test is the induction program. Online induction training sessions are a reality. This means that all processes and information need to be moved to an online platform if it's not already there. In the previous chapter, I suggested adding an integration stage to induction and onboarding. Cultivating two-way communication must be done online.

These sessions need to provide new employees with an opportunity to participate, ask questions, and share their expectations. Recruits may feel more uncomfortable asking questions online and building rapport with their new boss. Likewise, finding out more about the new employee's strengths and what they can bring to the business isn't any easier.

To encourage this online participation requires superior communication and interpersonal skills from leaders. In the digital world, it's ironic that people skills are even more relevant. The integration stage will undoubtedly be more challenging for employees working remotely. But paradoxically, integration is even more vital with physical separation. I'd suggest this isn't a good time to slash the communication and leadership development training budget!

Here are five other issues that need careful thought in a remote working environment.

First, it's even more important to contemplate what a new remote hire requires at every point of the onboarding journey. This includes before starting work, on the commencement of work, and in the first few months of employment. The process may vary from employee to employee too.

Second, how does the new employee receive feedback from their manager? As you're aware, feedback is minimal or nonexistent in the traditional workplace. But it's probably more trying in a remote situation. There are two types of feedback a new hire need. They need feedback about the company and its priorities. And there's the feedback around how the employee is settling into their day-to-day work. This is another reason to add an integration phase to the induction and onboarding program. These conversations can and should occur online.

Third, someone working remotely doesn't have the luxury (or misfortune!) of bumping into their boss in the corridor or lunchroom. These casual corridor conversations in the office offer opportunities to build working relationships. This prospect is lost working remotely. How does the manager develop a good rapport with their new team member, without incidental face-to-face contact?

Fourth, the presentation of important induction information needs rethinking. Generic videos from the CEO and long e-mails with lots of bullet points are probably not the solution.

And fifth, how does the remote worker create social bonds with their fellow workers? How can a new team member feel an integral part of the team? We understand that community is part of being human. Most employees working onsite spend more time with colleagues than their partners. How can the social dimension of a remote worker be fulfilled?

These questions are top-of-mind.

Improving employee engagement will continue to occupy the minds of HR. We need fresh perspectives on engagement at all stages of the employee lifecycle. People who work remotely need to feel sufficiently informed, valued, and appreciated. The reality is that most people working onsite don't feel informed, valued, and part of the team! So, it's likely that more and more remote workers will feel isolated and disengaged.

Improving workforce communications, apart from investing in new tools, is a part of engagement. Employees on average are spending approximately 2.5 hours a day on e-mail (Acton 2017).[9] This time includes reading, writing, and responding to online correspondence. As we know, this time isn't always fruitful, even though it must be done. I would urge HR professionals to read Cal Newport's book, *A World Without Email: Reimaging Work in an Age of Communication Overload.*[10] Newport has some great ideas that apply technology to manage projects. These project management tools move the hive of activity away from the relentless struggle to deal with our inbox.

Access to important information is another problem. The mantra, *out of sight out of mind* is very real with a dispersed workforce. And this is not remedied by a barrage of e-mails. Research shows that poor communication now costs companies a total of $37 billion every year (Schneider 2018).[11] So the cost of miscommunication will grow if companies don't implement digital alternatives. But these digital tools are only useful if the employee chooses to read the information.

It's not only interpersonal communication. What about training and development? About 67 percent of remote employees wish they had more access to work-related training.[12] Sharing information and improving the skills of remote workers helps them build and develop their capabilities.

Although online learning platforms are getting better, we need to make sure there is a balance between personal and professional development. I discuss training and development in more detail in Chapter 10.

And what about culture? With more of the workforce working remotely, how does this impact culture? Working remotely means that employees can often feel removed and not part of the company's culture. Sometimes this could be a good thing if the culture is poor! People working remotely get their cues of the way things are done from the touchpoints they have in their virtual interactions with colleagues and managers. Consistency of positive messages and the transferring of instrumental and terminal values we discussed in Chapter 1 becomes even more critical when employees are not in the office.

In conclusion, we must first accept the inevitable movement to hybrid working arrangements across many industries. And then we must address the issues I raised here.

In the next chapter, I want to discuss the collaborative employment relationship necessary to sustain the 13 mindset shifts.

Ten Key Takeaways

1. Although the subject of remote working isn't strictly a topic for the start-up phase of employment, effective ways of conveying information to and from offsite employees is increasingly becoming an issue.

2. Apart from productivity, there are other performance factors that should be discussed, whether working in an office or remotely.

3. Making the claim productivity is up or down working remote is too simplistic.

4. Pre-COVID, remote working arrangements were becoming more and more acceptable.

5. Although no one has all the answers, traditional management practices need to change faster to accommodate this shift.

6. Online induction training sessions are a reality. This means that all processes and information need to be moved to an online platform if it's not already there.

7. These sessions need to provide new employees with an opportunity to participate, ask questions, and share their expectations.

8. To encourage this online participation requires superior communication and interpersonal skills from leaders.
9. Improving employee engagement will continue to occupy the minds of HR.
10. Working remotely means that employees can often feel removed and not part of the company's culture.

CHAPTER 9

Shift 4: Them and Us to Collaboration

The major obstacle for organizational change is an outdated psychological contract, where employees still refer to management as *them* and themselves as *us*, and vice versa.

The newly appointed CEO in the government agency, Samantha, identifies as her first major challenge as breaking down the boundaries between departments. She observes that the agency is organized around several "silos"—it's a typically bureaucracy. This is evident even at the senior management level. The most important cross-functional team—the senior management team—is disjointed and not operating cohesively. Managers arrive at executive meetings with their functional "hat" on and fail to consider issues from the perspective of the overall organization. Samantha knows she has a problem and has her work cut out.

She notices the level of cooperation between departments is negligible, even non-existent, in some cases. Samantha is determined to change this. Instead of cooperation there is rivalry.

She decides to form several cross-functional project teams. One team is formed to look at improving communication across the agency, for example. Representatives are chosen by the new CEO from all six departments. Another cross-functional project team is set up to review and improve several archaic systems and processes that are not consistent across the agency.

Peter, from the marketing department, is invited by Samantha to be part of one of these project teams. He is enthusiastic about being asked to participate, recognizing the need to improve cross-functional communication throughout the organization. Peter goes to talk to the marketing manager in her office. Mary is apathetic when Peter tells her about this development.

"I wish the CEO had spoken to me first," Mary said to Peter in response to the news. "I can't afford to release you to attend these 'talk fests.' Peter, you are too valuable to the department. We're already short-staffed. How often does she want you to attend these meetings?"

"I don't know," replied Peter. "She hasn't told me yet."

"Well, it sounds like a complete waste of time. Your primary responsibility is to my department, Peter," said Mary. "You're a critical person in this department, and I'll have to speak to the CEO about this and let her know my feelings."

Peter left Mary's office deflated and confused. He'd thought this was a great opportunity to break down the silos in the agency and improve communication across the organization. He couldn't understand his boss's reaction. (Baker 2014)[1]

In the previous chapter, we looked at the challenges of working remotely. I now want to look at the mindset shift from a traditional manager–employee relationship to a collaborative relationship. Like all 13 mindset shifts, the employment relationship affects all phases of the employee lifecycle. The working relationship begins from the first day of work for the new hire.

Specifically, I want to look at eight shared beliefs that shape the employment relationship. The beliefs for the old and new employment relationship are diametrically opposite. These beliefs will provide a framework for change.

There is a commonly held view that we've made a successful transition from the traditional employment relationship. I'm not convinced that's true. I think a more accurate view is that most organizations are in transit between the old and the new employment relationship.

Without the new collaborative employment relationship as I describe it, many of the changes I'm suggesting in this book won't be sustainable.

If you're not familiar with the concept of the psychological contract, let me share with you what it is and how it impacts all HR practices. The concept of the psychological contract isn't new; it's been around for decades. I discuss it in detail in one of my previous books, *Breaking the*

Proactive Paradox: Maximizing Performance Through Empowerment.[2] However, in this chapter, I will summarize this work so that you're better able to understand the important shifts necessary to modernize the workplace.

Furthermore, a closer inspection of these 200 plus-year-old psychological contracts is useful to realize why the mindset shifts we're discussing are slow to change. The major obstacle for organizational change is an outdated psychological contract, where employees still refer to management as *them* and themselves as *us*, and vice versa.

Psychological Contract

What does the term *psychological contract* mean, and how is it relevant? A psychological contract can be defined as a set of unwritten expectations between employees and managers. Employees have a reasonably fixed set of beliefs about the role of management. And managers have certain generalized expectations of employees. In other words, a psychological contract is based on a set of beliefs both entities have about the role the other entity has in the relationship.

As a simple illustration, employees expect to be paid on time, be treated with respect, and be given a fair go by their manager. If employees don't believe their managers are upholding these basic expectations, from their perspective, the psychological contract has been breached. Management, in other words, has failed to live up to their side of the unwritten agreement and consequently infringed the contract.

On the other hand, managers have a customary expectation that employees will work hard, cause few problems, and arrive and leave work punctually. From the manager's perspective, if an employee's behavior is inconsistent with this, they have violated the contract. These beliefs (there are many more) have been handed down from generation to generation, with no real substantial change.

The traditional employment relationship—like all relationships—hinges on a set of shared beliefs between management and labor. A collaborating employment relationship is completely contrary to the old contract, as you'll see.

With a new contract, more workplace issues are dealt with cooperatively, where the drive for improvement is stronger than the fear of failure.

This shared leadership model is supported by an entirely different set of shared beliefs and expectations.

Even with the mantra we read about of a more collaboration between managers and employees, the characteristics of them & us affiliation is still prevalent to some extent in most contemporary businesses.

Where do most managers learn their management skills? From their managers. And who manages the managers? Those who were previously in those managers' roles. Likewise, employees learn from watching and listening to more experienced employees; they learn what to expect from management. With a long history, is it any wonder that these beliefs have remained static for so long?

I think it's helpful if I briefly summarize the contrasting beliefs in the two psychological contracts. I also want to consider these implications for some of the mindset shifts we are discussing.

Specialized Employment ⇒ Flexible Deployment

Specialized employment is the traditional belief that offering clearly defined and specialized employment opportunities is the best way to structure work in a stable and predictable marketplace. Narrow job specifications are easy for management to control—they are also easy for employees to follow.

Flexible deployment, on the other hand, is a belief that less structured and more adaptable employment opportunities are more suited in a VUCA marketplace. Leaders need to readily deploy people's skill sets to be agile in an ever-changing environment. Employees benefit too, by building a portfolio of capabilities for future career opportunities.

The belief of specialized employment impacts all four phases of the employee lifecycle. It shapes recruitment and selection practices with an obsession of finding a candidate with a track record of competency mastery. The belief narrows employee development to specialist roles. Specialized employment reinforces the relevance of the job specification and its cousin, the job description. It also promotes function-based work over project-based work. Specialized employment stifles succession planning by valuing technical leadership over people leadership. Appraising becomes more important than developing performance. And so on.

Internal-Focus ⇒ Customer-Focus

Internal focus is making sure that organizational processes and procedures are documented and adhered to. This emphasis is designed to improve organizational efficiency. This strategy is commonly referred to as quality assurance (QA). Like specialized employment, an internal focus enables managerial control. The manager impacts consistent outputs by prescribing the way things are done inside the business. There is an expectation that the employee will follows these set processes and procedures. While QA is undoubtedly important to produce quality products and services, an overreliance on internal quality means the business is less responsive to the ever-changing external marketplace.

A *customer-focus*, on the other hand, is concerned with equipping the employee with the necessary resources and information to deal effectively with the customer or end user.

The traditional belief in internal focus subjects the new hire to a plethora of systems and processes for how things should be done. Training needs are assessed on internal requirements. Job descriptions rarely state anything about the end users or customers. Function-based work limits communication between departments and external users. People are promoted based on their mastery of internal processes and procedures. And finally, when an employee leaves, little effort is made to stay connected with that employee.

Job Focus ⇒ Performance Focus

A *job-focus* is captured in the job description. Under the old contract, the employee performs their employment obligations when they fulfill the literal requirements of the job description. Here again, it's about management control. It's easier for the manager to supervise a narrow set of tasks and responsibilities the employee is prescribed to do. Adhering to the requirements of this document is sufficient in a stable and predictable marketplace, where people carry out series of repetitious tasks.

Performance-focus, on the other hand, considers both the job and nonjob requirements. Broadly, a performance-focus is doing what needs doing, rather than just following the obligations spelt out in the job description. I discuss these nonjob roles in detail in Chapter 11.

The belief around a job-focus reinforces the value of the job description and the job specification. More importantly, it underplays the importance of nonjob roles, multidimensional learning opportunities, and structuring organizations around specialized roles.

Function-Based Work ⇒ Project-Based Work

Function-based work refers to structuring labor in specialized departments. Clustering like-minded jobs together under the same roof has been conventional practice for a century and more.

Project-based work is structuring labor around projects. Although most businesses are organized around functional roles, most work-related tasks are accomplished cross-functionally. To be able to complete project work, people in departments communicate with people in other departments. Most complex work is project-based. The problem with functional structures is that jobholders only see a small part of a larger piece of work. This often leads to breakdowns in cross-functional communication. It makes sense therefore to view work as a series of projects rather than function based.

A project, with its distinctive processes and procedures, demands more collaboration than working in an organizational silo with its standard operating practices. The global pressures to be more responsive and agile to customer's requests add weight to the argument to shift from function-based to project-based working arrangements.

In Chapter 14, I discuss the rise of the super team and need for AI and humans to collaborate to produce exponential results. The concept of the super team requires a project-based rather than a functional-based mindset.

Human Dispirit and Work ⇒ Human Spirit and Work

Human dispirit and work is associated with jobs that are mundane and narrowly focused. This type of work has little scope for applying independent judgment. Job specification (see Chapter 13), the dominant work design model, typically creates jobs with a limited band of tasks and activities. These jobs are designed to simplify training needs, reduce costs, and minimize error rates. Job specification is prevalent across all industries—it therefore shouldn't be a surprise that surveys consistently show that more employees are disengaged than engaged in their work.

Human spirit and work, in contrast, is the belief that work—wherever possible—should be designed to be a meaningful experience for the employee. Work that is stimulating, reasonably challenging, and interesting, gives the employee more scope to be creative and exercise their autonomy to problem-solve. This type of work promises to be more engaging. Stimulating work with more variety has the potential to nourish one's human spirit, with opportunities to use their enterprising talents. We consider job crafting in Chapter 13 as a way to enhance job specification.

Apart from the impediments in employee development, human dispirit and work underpins the reward and punishment mentality that undercuts intrinsic motivation (Chapter 17).

Loyalty ⇒ Commitment

Loyalty in this context is faithfully adhering to the business's procedures and processes, without questioning its effectiveness. A loyal employee is highly valued in a work-setting that is steady and banal. By steadfastly upholding the way things *should* be done, the employee is fulfilling the manager's expectations in the old contract. A loyal employee is likely to stay with the company longer—sometimes too long!

Whereas loyalty is more process-driven, *commitment* is more outcome-driven.

Committing to achieving business results can involve thinking outside the box. An employee who faithfully follows a business's standard procedures doesn't have the right mindset to be enterprising, even when it's useful. On the other hand, committing to getting the work done opens the opportunity to think creatively and question the status quo.

This outdated notion of loyalty starts with the one-way induction and onboarding process. It stifles job crafting and cultivates a function-based rather than a project-based work mentality. Loyalty also impacts on succession planning. Proven technical leadership takes priority over people leadership. And finally, being loyal suggests that the employee should submit to an annual appraisal from their manager (Chapter 16).

Where the Rubber Meets the Road

Encouraging Work–Life Balance—Is It All Talk?

Most employers encourage a healthy work-life balance, but do they really mean what they say? One leading expert suggests too many companies offer nothing but lip-service.

"I have a large amount of cynicism around the sincerity of many companies," states Dr. Linda Duxbery, a management expert. "They talk balance but quite frankly they want people there and they want people working—it's shareholder value, its saving tax-payers' dollars."

According to Duxbery, "We've created a culture of the belief that the dedicated worker, the hard worker, the committed worker is the one who works the long hours and the people who push back are worried about getting ahead or even keeping their job in an environment like the one we have now."

But Duxbery acknowledges that this is probably going to change as millennials begin to make up most of the workforce. "They put a much higher priority on life," says Duxbery. "They've seen their parents on stress leave, they've seen their parents get divorced, they've seen their parents have drinking problems, on Prozac. They will not stay working for an organization that just gives lip service and doesn't provide balance." (Middlemiss 2015)[3]

Training ⇒ Learning and Development

Training emphasizes developing the jobholder's technical skills so they can better fulfill the requirements of their job. Training is primarily focused on improving job skills—it's still the dominant dimension of organizational learning. This hasn't changed in 100-years since the birth of scientific management. The main idea of scientific management is that there's *one best way* to do a job; and training will show you the way.

However, in the last 40 years, we've seen more emphasis on personal development and problem-based learning. Job skills training is still the main element of learning. *Learning and development* (L&D) is broader than training and includes the nontechnical aspects of learning. This belief accepts that personal development as an important dimension of employee development.

Personal development, problem-based, and machine-based learning (the three other dimensions of the L&D model I discuss in Chapter 10) assist the employee to be a more rounded and skilled decision maker. While training teaches a jobholder how to do a job task, it doesn't usually teach them to use independent judgment.

Closed Information ⇒ Open Information

Closed information is providing sufficient information—but no more—for the employee to complete the requirements of their current job. The old saying, *you'll get told on a need-to-know basis* is still heard today in the corridors of workplaces, unfortunately. The other common phrase we still hear is *no news is good news.*

Open information is the opposite. Open information is giving everyone access to a wide range of information beyond job needed. Opening the information channels gives the employee a similar perspective to their manager. Having a similar perspective is useful in a dynamic and rapidly changing workplace. A better-informed employee is likely to be more effective—they're more aware of when to seek their manager's input and when to think for themselves. In other words, they know when to bring their thoughts and ideas to the table, when to act autonomously, and to be able to choose between the two options.

I hope these descriptors help you to better understand the differences between the two psychological contracts. Although contrasting, identifying the variations in the contracts gives you a more thorough grasp of the changes necessary to facilitate a collaborative working relationship. The new contract is the cornerstone for the 13 mindset shifts.

This brings us to the end of PART 2. In PART 3 we discuss five mindset shifts necessary in the developing phase of the employee lifecycle. We begin with the shift from training to multidimensional learning.

Ten Key Takeaways

1. The employment relationship affects all phases of the employee lifecycle.
2. A psychological contract can be defined as a set of unwritten expectations between employees and managers.
3. Flexible deployment is a belief that less structured and more adaptable employment opportunities are more suited in a VUCA marketplace.
4. A customer-focus is concerned with equipping the employee with the necessary resources and information to deal effectively with the customer or end user.
5. A performance-focus is doing what needs doing, rather than just following the obligations spelt out in the job description.
6. Project-based work is structuring labor around projects.
7. Human spirit and work is the belief that work—wherever possible—should be designed to be a meaningful experience for the employee.
8. Committing to achieving business results can involve thinking outside the box.
9. L&D is broader than training and includes the nontechnical aspects of learning.
10. Open information is giving everyone access to a wide range of information beyond job needed.

PART 3

Developing Phase of Employment

CHAPTER 10

Shift 5: Training to Multidimensional Learning

There's rarely a neat, prescriptive answer to resolving complex, left-field problems. The answers aren't always going to be found in the company procedure's manual.

Julie—executive manager of learning and development (L&D) for a large, well-known bank—was charged with the responsibility of revamping the bank's approach to inducting customer service representatives (CSRs) in retail banking services. After looking at the turnover rates and gathering information from a series of conversations she had with CSRs and their managers, she decided it was time to act.

From what she'd heard in these conversations, the bank had a challenge to reduce the high rates of turnover in CSRs in the first 12 weeks of their employment with the bank. Employees had told Julie in their conversations that they lacked confidence in their skills and product knowledge. Changing the learning approach in the induction program was the place to start, she concluded. Most of this training had in the past been too prescriptive and procedural and hadn't considered the ambiguous circumstances CSRs were often put in on the job. From a learning perspective, the new approach enabled participants to better analyze situations and source information more effectively. This policy, supported by a continuous coaching component, involved a partnership between the participant, their branch manager, and a "buddy" who was an experienced CSR. With this support, participants were required to take ownership of their learning and complete a series of tasks. In addition, they worked with their branch manager to identify strengths and areas of improvement through daily check-ins, debriefs, and feedback sessions.

Collaborative learning occurs using problem-based learning, simulations, and research. During the off-the-job learning periods, participants work in learning sets or groups and explore customer situations that they'd encounter in real life. They were encouraged to analyze the situation, explore how they would respond, and complete any customer transactions using simulations.

To date, the CSR induction program has been able to deliver an 8 percent reduction in voluntary turnover in the first six months of its inception. (Baker 2014)[1]

Once the new hire has passed through the starting phase of the employee lifecycle, they are exposed to the company's L&D program. In this chapter, we look at the traditional way that the employee is developed. More than ever, people need to be exposed to a variety of L&D opportunities. In the previous chapter, one of the beliefs in the employment relationship that needed a shift in thinking was to move from a dominant training focus to a broader L&D approach. A multidimensional approach better prepares the employee for a world of uncertainty and unpredictability.

The success of scientific management substantially relied upon teaching workers to comply with the one and only way of carrying out their job. Training was based on how to do a job. In the early days of scientific management, nontechnical development programs were nonexistent and considered irrelevant. But today L&D programs that aren't job-specific are commonplace, although still substantially overshadowed by job training.

Technical mastery of the job is still the dominant form of learning, even though work performance extends past the boundaries of the job specification, as we discussed in PART 1. Technical job skills training isn't the panacea for all performance issues. An overreliance on job-centered training discounts nontechnical L&D options.

An agile enterprise needs more than job skill development to perform in a turbulent marketplace. Technical mastery is still important, of course. With technical training closely aligned with specialization and standardization of work, it's understandable why it remains the dominant mode of learning in workplaces. No one can seriously dispute its value in a high-performing workplace. But nontechnical proficiency is increasingly vital.

> The most sought-after skills of the future are not technical, but behavioral; those so-called soft skills, or as we should be calling them, power skills. So says Corporate Talent, HR, and Learning Analyst, Josh Bersin. We know from recent studies that digital and technical skills will be important to businesses of the future. Bersin says, "More than 45% of chief human resource officers tell us people coming out of college have the digital skills they need. What they are missing is skills in complex problem solving, teamwork, business understanding, and leadership."[2]

Across the spectrum of industries, employees are faced with a daily bombardment of problems, challenges, and dilemmas. Many of these predicaments can't be fixed with procedural knowledge and process skills learnt from technical training. Thinking outside the box is the new norm. There's rarely a neat, prescriptive answer to resolving complex, left-field problems. The answers aren't always going to be found in the company procedure's manual.

More and more of these out-of-the-blue challenges facing people at work require thinking on one's feet. Job training doesn't teach people to think laterally. Essentially, job training does the opposite—it teaches trainees to follow procedures, processes, and systems. A key assumption supporting job learning is that work situations are reasonably predictable and so can be resolved in a particular way, using a specific method. This idea is at the heart of scientific management and the stable and predictable marketplace it was borne out of.

What's the Difference Between Training and L&D?

Training is one dimension of L&D. In other words, training is one of several approaches to L&D. Furthermore, its primary focus is to improve the job capabilities of the jobholder. L&D is broader and includes both the technical and nontechnical dimensions of learning. Being more

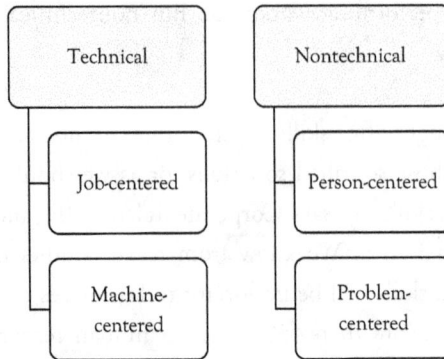

Figure 10.1 Multidimensional learning model

comprehensive, L&D covers all the people development practices essential for building and sustaining individual and organizational agility.

My multidimensional learning model shown in Figure 10.1 consists of four dimensions. Job skills is one dimension. Its focus is technical. Machine-based, problem-based, and personal development are the three other dimensions. Training, digital, personal development, and problem-solving skills make up the multidimensional learning model.

Technical, in this instance, refers to job-related learning. Nontechnical is L&D that indirectly impacts one's capacity to do the job. Each of the four dimensions has an apparent focus in its application. Briefly, the job-centered dimension focuses on technical job training. The machine-centered dimension is the other technical dimension concerned with mastering digital capabilities. The person- and problem-centered dimensions are nontechnical in their orientation. Person-centered is concerned with learning personal and interpersonal skills. Problem-centered learning focuses on building capacity to diagnose and solve problems. Together, the four dimensions make up the multidimensional learning model needed for agile performance.

Let's take a closer look at each of the four dimensions.

Job-Centered

The most popular and conventional method overwhelmingly adopted by most organizations is *job-centered*. I'd guess 60 percent or more of learning activities carried out in most organizations could be classified as job-centered.

This dimension emphasizes technical performance and skill mastery. The justification for expending money on building technical capacity is the tangible link between the jobholder and their job performance.

So, its primary motive is to develop the employee's job skills to directly improve performance on-the-job. Of the four dimensions, the job-centered approach is the one most related to the specifics of one's job performance.

Training programs, for instance, that explain a work-related system or process or learning a skill such as writing a report are job-centered. These activities specifically relate to a job task. These training programs are job-centered in their orientation. Successfully learning anything straight from a jobholder's job description has a direct pay-off in their increased job performance.

Quality learning programs that are job-specific increase the employee's efficiency and effectiveness in their job role. The ultimate triumph of job-centered training is a more technically proficient employee. It's obvious therefore why most enterprises invest heavily in job-centered training programs.

The employee benefits too, of course. Being technically proficient makes one's job easier and reduces stress levels. Technical training assists an employee in performing their job with greater confidence and increased competence, in other words. And improved job performance can lead to promotion and more pay—job-centered training can benefit one's career.

Despite its popularity, it primarily favors the interests of the organization over the interests of the employee. The dominant job-centered training approach applied in most companies is based on Taylorism thinking; that is, the employee is a small cog in the large-scale wheel of production. The employee is viewed as an abstract and anonymous jobholder or performer.

The overriding expectation is for the jobholder undertaking job-centered training is to follow a prescribed task. There's little scope for original thought or independent judgment.

As I pointed out, it's true that the employee gains new skills that can benefit them and their career. But job-centered training is first and foremost about boosting the business.

Machine-Centered

Of increasing importance is *machine-centered* learning. As technology and AI infiltrates our lives, people need digital mastery. The boundaries between job-centered and machine-centered learning are becoming increasingly blurred. They are both technical in their orientation. But job-centered training is more about learning to follow systems and processes and machine-centered learning is specific to mastering the skills of operating a piece of machinery or technology.

This dimension emphasizes the technical performance of working with AI and technology that's necessary for the jobholder to do their job successfully.

The justification for expending money on building digital capacity is again the tangible link between the jobholder and their job performance.

This dimension helps the employee to directly improve performance on-the-job. So, like job-centered learning, machine-centered mastery is related to the specifics of one's job performance.

Any training program that assists a jobholder to operate a piece of machinery that they need to use in carrying out their duties and responsibilities, now or in the future, fall under this category. This includes collaborating with AI, both individually and within teams. I explain this context further in Chapter 14.

This technical training, like the job-centered dimension, enhances an employee's capacity to be successful as a jobholder. They boost their technical proficiency, in other words. It is likely that companies will continue to invest in machine-centered learning for the future.

There is an obvious benefit for the employee in this type of learning. It enables them to broaden their array of skills to enhance future career prospects. But again, the primary motive is to improve organizational performance now and in the future.

Person-Centered

The *person-centered* approach emphasizes self-development; it involves the employer investing in the personal growth of its employees, as people.

This dimension of learning has a less direct link between the learning experience and job and organizational performance. Job-centered learning is directly connected to job performance. And machine-centered learning is tied to organizational performance. The person-centered approach is more concerned with developing the individual.

The motive for an enterprise sponsoring person-centered development is basically the same as the job- and machine-centered approaches with a different impact. With person-centered learning, the approach is designed to develop certain personal qualities that can ultimately improve their work performance. Unlike the job- and machine-centered approaches, however, person-centered learning can indirectly—rather than directly—influence job and business performance. The person-centered approach is based on the idea that a more accomplished person can be a more accomplished employee.

Programs that improve an employee's mastery of themselves—rather than mastery of a job skill or machine capability—such as resilience training, enhancing emotional intelligence, and time management, potentially increase work performance in particular ways.

The incentive for an enterprise to sponsor personal development learning opportunities is to grow and nurture abler employees. Furthermore, it's based on the belief that by developing the organization's more precious resource—its people—employees can be more efficient and effective in their work role. Over the past quarter of a century, the proliferation of personal development experiences, courses, and activities suggest this premise is well-founded.

Aside from the firm, the people undertaking these programs can benefit the most. The opportunity to develop and enrich their life and career prospects is appealing to most people. Personal development broadens their range of skills past technical capabilities. Despite its growing popularity, it's still a less appealing investment for HR than job-centered training. This is mainly due to the weaker connection between the learning experience and job performance.

There's a subtle similarity between job-, machine-, and person-centered approaches. This connection is relevant when the business is the sponsor. A person-centered learning experience is pursued—like the job- and machine-centered approaches—in the interests of the paying organization foremost. The employee's needs—although not necessarily obvious on the surface—are a secondary consideration, in most cases. It's common practice for an employee, attending a personal development training program, to follow unquestioningly the direction of a trainer and their prescribed program. The course content is usually set in advance, with the trainer follows a predetermined pathway, regardless of the specific needs of the program's attendees.

It's typically the case that the trainee is given little option but to simply follow what the trainer says. Despite the rhetoric of "self-discovery," there is generally no real opportunity for the *participant* to engage in any real independent thinking in personal development programs. The trainee merely reacts to the direction set by the trainer and faithfully follows the sequence of activities in the training manual. Many personal development courses—like technical training programs—are "how to" or procedurally driven learning experiences.

Take for example, a *Five Steps to Better Listening* communication program. The trainer typically leads the workshop participant methodically through these five steps—as entertaining and informative as it may be— throughout the duration of the program. I've no doubt this approach has merit. Procedural knowledge gained this way is valuable and necessary for some life skills.

However, too much attention on procedural training, undercuts the capacity for real personal development. So, in more circumstances than may first appear obvious, the person-centered approach undermines the individual's fundamental and inherent self-determination.

Notwithstanding the organization-centric nature of job-, machine-, and person-centered programs, they are valuable and certainly have an ongoing role in the performance-oriented enterprise. But these three dimensions and their programs reinforce the idea that the employer's needs take precedence over the needs of the employee.

Problem-Centered

The *problem-centered* approach, the fourth dimension of the multidimensional learning model, is based on problem-solving; that is, being more effective at solving work-related problems. The focus here is developing the employee's ability to analyze and resolve problems at work.

With more capable problem-solving skills, people can make better decisions on-the-job. The argument for using this learning method is this: by improving an employee's decision-making aptitude, they improve their performance. By coping more effectively with the escalating and unpredictable challenges they face in their work, the employee is better able to do their job. People can make better decisions in their day-to-day work if they have the necessary knowledge, skills, and attitude to deal with random problems, challenges, and dilemmas.

Also, with greater problem-solving capabilities, employees exercise greater autonomy in dealing with ambiguous issues affecting their work. This increased independence reduces the employee's dependency on their supervisor.

Topics such as creative problem-solving techniques, research skills, or analysis of real-world case studies are examples of problem-centered learning. In their recent book *The Curious Advantage*, Paul Ashcroft, Simon Brown, and Garrick Jones state that, "Curiosity is the greatest driver of value in the new digital age. Curiosity is at the heart of the skills required to successfully navigate our digital lives when all futures are uncertain." I agree. It remains a mystery to me why this approach isn't more rampant in workplaces. When you consider the obvious relevance of problem-solving today, why isn't there more of this type of learning?

When applied, this dimension of learning is based on the belief that by developing people's problem-solving capacity, it stimulates a faster and more considered decision. It also encourages lateral thinking.

Like the other three dimensions of learning, the employee benefits from building better problem-solving capabilities. An incentive to learn to deal with problems is to be more autonomous. The employee is going to be less reliant on their boss to make decisions affecting their work. I'll pick up on this theme in Chapter 17 in the rewarding phase of the employee lifecycle.

Learning to problem-solve also enhances a person's employability prospects. Although slow to take hold—even with its obvious benefits— problem-centered learning experiences are gradually gaining prominence.

The complex and less predictable working environment we face guarantee its ascendancy.

Where the Rubber Meets the Road

Thinking Outside the Box

Southwest's senior vice president for corporate communication, Ginger Hardage, told participants at a conference a story about a Southwest pilot:

"On September 11, 2001, after terrorists had brought the twin towers down, all planes that were already in the air were grounded. A Southwest plane was directed to land at an airport that Southwest did not serve, and the passengers and crew were put up in a hotel. When Southwest management called the hotel to enquire about the passengers and crew, they were told that no one was there—the pilot had taken everyone from that plane out to the movies."

"There's no manual from which to learn that" said Hardage. "At Southwest, employees are encouraged to make decisions from the heart, and in turn, these proactive gestures provide positive benefits to the customers and the company." (Baker 2009)[3]

Toward a Multidimensional Approach

The problem-centered approach should be jointly considered and applied with the job-, machine-, and person-centered perspectives. In the working environment we participate in, the ability to think laterally, creatively, and flexibly is paramount. Intense global competition puts pressure on treating every customer's request as exclusively as possible. This entails abandoning stock standard problem-solving approaches that frustrate the fickle customer. Being able to take an extraordinary situation and deal with it proficiently is a skills-set that benefits everyone: the customer, employee, and company.

There are strong advocates with compelling arguments for each of the four L&D approaches. And that's fine—they all have their place in the learning landscape. But each approach has its limitations too. So, it stands to reason that the best L&D strategy for companies to adopt is multidimensional. An eclectic strategy, being comprehensive, brings to light the value of each perspective.

Choosing from a range of different perspectives to solve performance issues has a broader set of options than simply defaulting to job-centered skills training. HR boosts their odds of resolving performance problems in the business by adopting a multidimensional approach to L&D.

Before you claim that you use all four in your company, consider this: What percentage of your learning programs are job-centered, machine-centered, person-centered, and problem-centered? To truly shift from the mindset of training to multidimensional learning, I suggest that one quarter of an organization's L&D budget should be allocated to each of the four dimensions.

Ten Key Takeaways

1. Technical mastery of the job is still the dominant form of learning, even though work performance extends past the boundaries of the job specification.
2. An agile enterprise needs more than job skill development to perform in a turbulent marketplace.
3. Training is one dimension of L&D.
4. The multidimensional learning model consists of four dimensions: job-, machine-, person-, and problem-centered.
5. Job-centered learning emphasizes technical performance and skill mastery.
6. Machine-centered learning emphasizes the technical performance of working with AI and technology that's necessary for the jobholder to do their job successfully.
7. Person-centered learning emphasizes self-development.
8. Problem-centered learning is based on problem-solving.
9. Choosing from a range of different perspectives to solve performance issues has a broader set of options than simply defaulting to job-centered skills training.
10. One quarter of an organization's L&D budget should be allocated to each of the four dimensions.

CHAPTER 11

Shift 6: Job to Nonjob Roles

Performing at work goes well beyond the piece of paper we refer to as a job description.

Results from the Leadership Pulse study conducted by the Ross School of Business indicate that by spending more time on "non-core job roles," organizations might see higher levels of overall performance. This is especially true within those companies that have fewer than 500 employees. Respondents included 378 senior executives, managers, and leaders, who were assessed on five performance-based roles. These roles have been found to be critical for understanding overall, individual, and company performance and include:

- Job: reflects the basic core job one is hired to perform and is often well described in the typical job description.
- Team: reflects responsibilities for ongoing and project-based teams.
- Career: includes responsibilities to enhance career and skills.
- Innovator: covers work spent to develop new ideas, create new routines, or improve on process.
- Organization member: reflects work done to support company overall, when it's not part of the other roles.[1]

In the previous chapter, we discussed the multidimensional learning model, covering four dimensions of L&D. The main point was to ensure that all four dimensions are part of the development phase of the employee lifecycle. I want to now turn your attention to developing performance and the increasing importance of nonjob roles.

Performing at work goes well beyond the piece of paper we refer to as a job description. People can play a multitude of roles at work, apart from their job role. As I point out in my book, *The End of the Job Description:*

Shifting from a Job-focus to a Performance-focus,[2] we need to abandon the job description and replace it with a role description. I'll get to that in the next chapter.

In this chapter, I want to identify and define four important nonjob roles that impact performance. By developing these four roles, we can significantly impact business performance. These four nonjob roles can be cultivated with the assistance of person- and problem-centered learning experiences. With more emphasis on these nonjob roles there is mindset shift from job to nonjob roles.

The pervasive influence of the job description distorts the nonjob dimension of work to irrelevance in performance development. This is despite our instinctive understand of the value certain attitudes and behaviors have on workplace success. What's more, nonjob roles are becoming more and more relevant to propel business toward the adaptive advantage necessary now.

So ubiquitous is the job description in the employee lifecycle, it's used to justify sacking someone, even for unrelated matters. The job description provides legal cover for the disgruntled manager. While managers use poor performance measured against the KPIs in the job description as the basis for termination of someone's employment, it's often-other issues. Ironically, it's dreadful nonjob behavior that's often the real reason for dismissal. There's no doubting the influence of the job description—it guides and informs every aspect of the employee lifecycle, ranging from recruitment to termination.

Academics have been paying attention to nonjob roles for decades. They have been slow to nominate the generic nonjob roles that are applicable for all industries, however. I have decided to bite the bullet and identify four nonjob roles that are critical for success in all industries. These nonjob roles therefore need more attention in employee development.

Model of Work Performance

By elevating these significant nonjob roles and developing them, performance in the modern setting will undoubtedly be boosted. Indeed, the same rigor we apply to job performance criteria should be applied to nonjob performance. I acknowledge that some companies do, to some extent, address these nonjob roles. But generally, they aren't given the same attention as technical capability.

Mostly, nonjob roles are expressed in vague statements such as: *We encourage employees to offer their suggestions at work*; or perhaps more directly: *You are expected to be a team player.* Either way, nonjob role descriptors—if they are included at all—are listed after the task-specific job details, at the end of the job description. Furthermore, there's an absence of detail on how they will be measured. Nonjob behaviors are open to misinterpretation.

The development of these nonjob roles promotes a more comprehensive performance framework. This holistic interpretation of performance covers both job and nonjob behaviors. The nonjob performance framework that I will discuss shortly supports and reinforces desirable workplace accomplishment that isn't job specific. What's more, I want to overhaul the key deficiency in the performance management system—the job description—and replace it with a role description that covers both the job and nonjob roles.

Figure 11.1 illustrates the model of work performance.

As you can see, there are two dimensions to performance—job and nonjob. The job role is described in the job description. As I stated in the last chapter, training largely covers the technical aspects of a jobholder's development. You will notice that there are four nonjob roles in the framework.

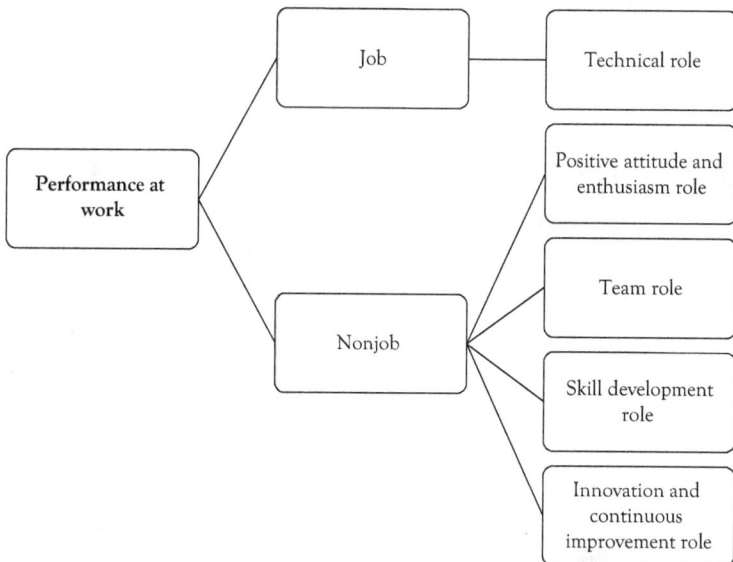

Figure 11.1 Model of work performance

There are undoubtedly many other roles—apart from the four in the model—that contribute to personal and organizational success. But these four roles are undeniably applicable in all industries and work contexts.

I will define these four nonjob roles in the model of performance and explain why they need to be elevated and developed.

Two of the nonjob roles in the framework are *interpersonal* and the other two are *personal*.

Where the Rubber Meets the Road

How Organizations Should Approach Growth

According to *The Employee Expectations Report 2021*, for growth to be reimagined, organizations need to take the following actions:

Develop Manager Coaching Skills

The best people leaders know how to facilitate the growth of their team through coaching. But very few people develop these skills naturally. In fact, one study of over 3,000 executives found that 24 percent significantly overestimated their abilities when rated based on colleagues' feedback. Coaching enables managers and employees to work together in a way that uncovers opportunities for growth that might not be obvious—especially during a time when most promotions and pay rises have been frozen.

Support More Virtual and Peer-to-Peer Learning

Despite a lack of progression opportunities, organizations can still help employees to develop skills that will benefit their future career. Virtual learning makes this a much more affordable (and accessible) option compared to traditional classroom learning, while peer-to-peer learning taps into the wealth of knowledge already available within your organization. You could even support employees who want to develop skills outside of the professional realm to develop trust and loyalty.

Outline a Clear Post-COVID Development Plan

As the world returns to some form of normality, so too will the number of opportunities outside of your organization. Employees that feel they have stagnated during the pandemic will have little reason to stay, which is why it's essential to provide high performers with a clear development plan. Failing to do so will only contribute to higher levels of turnover and increased hiring costs. (Peakon 2021)[3]

Interpersonal Nonjob Roles

I'll define the positive attitude and enthusiasm role first. It's impossible to be positive and enthusiastic all the time at work, or anywhere else for that matter. But equally, being negative and lacking enthusiasm, all the time is impossible too. Although I have met some people that test this proposition! One's attitude affects those close to them. And that's why I've categorized this role as interpersonal, though one's attitude is a personal choice.

I think it's reasonable to expect everyone working together in a business to be positive and enthusiastic most of the time. Research shows that being enthusiastic and positive is regarded as the most important attribute managers are looking for in employees (Warner 2012).[4] With the relentless pressure for companies to rapidly chop and change, being positive is essential for building and maintaining morale through these unyielding and demoralizing disruptions.

People at work have for some time been expected to *do more with less* and this adds another layer of pressure on the working environment. Add to this increased competition, the snowballing fixation for *dotting i's and crossing t's*, the burdens of excessive accountability, and the need to be transparent. This all leads to heightened stress levels.

Maintaining a positive attitude can be an antidote for these pressures and stresses. What's more, cultivating a harmonious working environment is a priceless commodity today. So, it's unsurprising with all these 360-degree stresses and strains on the business, that attitude and enthusiasm is so highly valued.

Although developing a positive attitude is a personal responsibility, if companies don't elevate its importance, people will assume that it's not that important.

Being a "team player" is the other interpersonal nonjob role in the model. With the erosion of hierarchy and the corresponding flattening of organizational structures, teams are now the main organizing work structure. I cover this in some detail in Chapter 14.

Having team awareness is another sought-after attribute. Employees are increasingly participating in short- and long-term project teams; often with people they have never met, let alone worked with before. Many of these teams work remotely. These cross-functional project teams are often hastily formed to solve problems or deal with arising issues. This was very evident during 2020. These teams comprise members with a diverse array of perspectives and expertise. Working harmoniously and constructively will continue to be a valuable employee asset.

Being able to work in a team is one of the top 10 sought-after employee attributes (Warner 2012).[5] Managers recognize, understandably, that effectively cooperating with others is critical to success. However, playing a team role isn't as simple as it sounds—it's a complex mix of skill, knowledge, and attitude.

A team player needs, for instance, to be:

- Capable and willing of influencing colleagues and simultaneously be open to the influence of their team members.
- Able to juggle the dual responsibilities of team and individual outputs.
- Able to work cooperatively and harmoniously with others under duress.
- Ready and able to interact and exchange information with a variety of stakeholders.

Despite its complexity, the ability to work in a team environment benefits organizations, managers, and employees. Team development programs (person-centered approach) should therefore be a priority for companies if it isn't already.

Personal Nonjob Roles

The first of the two personal nonjob roles—the skill development role—is concerned with the continual growth and development of the employee technically and personally. Committing to lifelong learning is essential for individual career and organization success. Continually improving, upgrading, and expanding one's skill base and developing personally, benefits not only the person but their current and future employer in the transforming world of work.

Though we've all met people who have stopped learning and developing in their working life. When challenged, a stagnant employee often gives a lame excuse like, *I'm too old to learn anything new*, or when offered a career development opportunity, they retort with, *I'm just happy doing what I have always done.*

There are two aspects to the skill development role. One relates to the job or technical development (job-centered approach). In essence, this involves making career decisions about education, training, and career options. The second aspect is about self-development (person-centered). Self-development involves improving oneself to indirectly assist in carrying out employment responsibilities.

Personal development can cover such things, for instance, as managing time and priorities more effectively, developing "people skills," and reducing stress levels. Exercising the skill development role—like the other nonjob roles—has benefits personally and interpersonally.

The skill development role reinforces the need for all four dimensions of the multidimensional learning model I discussed in the last chapter.

The final of the four nonjob roles in the model of work performance and the second of the personal nonjob roles is the innovation and continuous improvement role. While the skill development role is about improving the individual, the innovation and continuous improvement role is concerned with improving the workplace.

This role is about offering constructive and timely suggestions and changes in how the business can function better. Innovation and continuous improvement can cover a wide spectrum of things in the workplace. For instance, it may include:

- Improving the quality products or services.
- Reducing the time and cost of production, without sacrificing quality.
- Increasing output.
- Minimizing accidents and enhancing safety.

- Improving responsiveness and meeting deadlines.
- Enhancing interpersonal cooperation and improving channels of communication.
- Streamlining systems and processes.

For business to prosper in a VUCA world—like the employee—it needs to be engaged in an endless state of growth and development. All employees should have a role to play in this regard. Elevating the importance of the innovation and continuous improvement role can be achieved with development opportunities in the dimensions of person- and problem-centered learning.

By exercising these four nonjob roles, the employee's performance is extended to fulfilling their organizational role beyond their job role. From an organization development perspective, the nonjob roles the employee performs well, not too well, or poorly, impacts the performance of the enterprise. It's widely acknowledged that roles such as preserving a positive and enthusiastic attitude, exhibiting teamwork, improving one's work skills, and contributing to the betterment of the functioning of the workplace are key to organizational performance. And yet these four attributes are nonjob-specific and as such, are rarely—if ever—covered sufficiently in an employee's job description. They are therefore neglected or not given the attention they deserve during the development phase of the employee lifecycle. This shifts the focus from the job to nonjob roles.

In the next chapter, we look at recrafting the job description to a role description to accommodate these four nonjob roles.

Ten Key Takeaways

1. People can play a multitude of roles at work, apart from their job role.
2. The pervasive influence of the job description distorts the nonjob dimension of work to irrelevance in performance development.
3. The development of these nonjob roles promotes a more comprehensive performance framework.
4. Two of the nonjob roles in the framework are interpersonal and the other two are personal.

5. The first interpersonal nonjob role in the model is the positive attitude and enthusiasm role.

6. The second interpersonal role is the team role.

7. The first personal role is the skill development role.

8. The second personal role is the innovation and continuous improvement role.

9. By exercising these four nonjob roles, the employee's performance is extended to fulfilling their organizational role beyond their job role.

10. These four attributes are nonjob-specific and as such, are rarely—if ever—covered sufficiently in an employee's job description.

CHAPTER 12

Shift 7: Job Description to Role Description

By transitioning from a job to role description, the employer is acknowledging explicitly the totality of the employee's organizational contribution.

Maryanne, a new customer service officer was being inducted and trained by Felicity, a long-time member of a customer service team. The new employee appreciated her trainer's experience and knowledge and quickly gained a level of confidence in her new job. One thing she also quickly learned was that a key performance measure in her new job description was how rapidly visitors were processed, not how well their inquiries were handled.

"It feels like churn and burn," Maryanne told her trainer. "Lots of these people are coming back again and again with the same issue and they're upset at us for not giving them the right information. It seems like we should be spending more time finding out what the real issue is when they first come in."

"Not our problem," said Felicity in response to Maryanne's protest. "That's the manager's problem. They just don't want to see lines of people." "Besides, it doesn't say anything about spending more time than necessary in your job description, does it?" "Go with what's in your job description and you can't go wrong, Maryanne," advised the trainer.

Although Maryanne wasn't content with this response, as a new employee, she persevered with things until she took complete ownership of the job and then started engaging in richer conversations with customers to solve their issues more effectively. Maryanne also rationalized that by doing so, she would minimize repeat visits and provide better customer service.

"You're taking too long with the customers," she was told by Royce, her manager, after a month on the job. Explaining her rationale and commitment to delivering a better service was to no avail.

"That's not your concern," she was told by Royce. (Baker 2016)[1]

Excelling at a job and performing at work are not necessarily the same. Plenty of jobholders are doing what's required of them based on their job description but failing to perform. You can be meticulously covering all the KRAs in our job description, and still underachieve. On the other hand, it's possible to be getting good results without necessarily following the exact requirements specified in the job description. As we discussed in the previous chapter, nonjob roles are underrated because they don't carry the same status as the job role. The job description is mainly concerned with the job rather than nonjob roles.

In this chapter, we'll consider how the job description has a detrimental effect during the development phase of the employee lifecycle. For this reason, it's time to shift from a job description to role description.

To reinforce what I said in the last chapter: Performing is more than completing the tasks cited in the job description. We considered four important nonjob roles that can make or break any organization, regardless of the technical proficiency of the workforce. Before explaining how to transition from a job description to a role description, let's consider the harmful impact the job description has on people development in all phases of the employee lifecycle.

Unless the new employee is recruited internally, the first contact HR has with a new employee is during the selection process, typically in an interview. And as we know, the conventional practice of selecting the suitable candidate centers on the job-related criteria in the job description. But we also know that this method can backfire with disastrous consequences. As I argue in Chapter 6, if HR don't broaden the selection criteria beyond job competencies, it's not hiring for future potential.

Putting aside potential, here is a typical illustration of neglecting factors beyond job competencies: After the probationary period lapsed, Lisa— one of the selection panelists— turns to Rod, another on the panel and says, with a rueful expression, "If only we had known that Bill (the new employee) would treat everyone with contempt and disrespect when we interviewed him several months ago." "If only!" repeats Rod with a sigh.

In the quest to find the more technically competent candidate, non-job attributes are often overlooked. Attitude and enthusiasm, the ability to work constructively with a variety of colleagues and stakeholders, the candidate's readiness to develop personally and technically, and their pre-paredness to question the status quo, are often bypassed. Although the successful candidate ticks the box on job competency, they can disappoint on the job.

In fairness, sometimes these (and other) nonjob attributes are con-sidered in the recruitment and selection process. But even when they are contemplated, they're of secondary importance to their technical compe-tency. The selection panel typically makes some assumptions about the candidate's ability to fulfill these nonjob roles. But by-and-large, the panel are pressured by HR to stick to the script; that is, the focus is on technical qualifications embedded in the job description.

For consistency and fairness, the selection process asks the same set of questions to each candidate and the referees of the successful applicant. By doing this, it reinforces the primacy of job functions in the selection criteria. With consistent responses from the referees, the favored candi-date is offered the job. The status of nonjob roles is already diminishing even before the new hire commences their new job.

This sends a signal in the starting phase of the employee lifecycle that nonjob roles don't need development. This assumption is further rein-forced when the employee commences their new job. Once the selection ritual is over, the new employee commences their new job. Most new employees, particularly those recruited from outside the organization, are understandably a mix of excitement and apprehension on day one. This early stage of the employment cycle is a golden opportunity to positively shape and mold a set of productive habits at work, or at least break old, unhelpful habits in a new employee.

During the induction and onboarding process, there is a strong emphasis on preparing the new employee to undertake their job role. Less emphasis is placed on expectations around nonjob behavior. This orien-tation further entrenches the significance of job tasks. And from the early stages of induction, the new employee can be forgiven for thinking that nonjob roles are comparatively insignificant to their employment success.

A good leader sits down with a new team member during the first few weeks of employment and discusses their expectations regarding nonjob performance. This is done to prepare them for the various roles they are expected to play, apart from their job role. But alas, as we know, good leaders are in short supply. This is another reason for suggesting an integration phase in the induction and onboarding stage.

In most cases, the new employee's supervisor was involved in their selection; and that process—in all probability—focused exclusively on job-related competencies. The subsequent task-specific interaction further reinforces the impression that the nonjob roles people play at work are of less relevance and importance.

As the employee passes the probationary period, they are exposed to training and development opportunities. Most of these learning opportunities, as I pointed out in Chapter 10, are technical training programs designed to improve their current and future job competencies. Training programs that build nonjob competencies, such as team development, are more prevalent than they once were, but less prominent than job competency development.

Here again, the job description and its technical focus shapes L&D offerings. Technical training designed to improve job-specific competencies has been the conventional approach to employee development since the birth of industry. Training with this technical orientation helps employees develop their skills-set to do their job with more capability. Although technical training is unquestionably essential, as I've stated in Chapter 10, companies and employees need more than technical skills and know-how to survive and prosper in the rapidly changing marketplace.

However, hypercompetition and the rapidly changing and unpredictable marketplace has elevated the importance of being able to solve unique and challenging problems and displaying initiative, sometimes on the spur-of-the-moment. Person-centered and problem-centered learning opportunities become more relevant.

Like the starting and developing, the reward phase of the employee lifecycle sidesteps the development of nonjob skills. Remuneration and promotional decisions are colored by the job description. Assessing the pay levels of employees is never an easy task. When it comes to evaluating pay rises, we again tend to rely on the strict letter of the job description to inform our decision. This is done under the guise of fairness and impartiality.

It's considered too risky to stray beyond the confines of the six to eight KRAs in the job description to make judgments about whether to give an employee a pay rise. To judge other factors apart from the job description is thought to be too subjective. Leaders' image of themselves as objective decision makers is misguided, however.

Succession planning is the practice of identifying and developing people in the enterprise with the potential to fill key business leadership positions in the future. As with the other HR practices, the job description has an unhealthy sway on succession planning decisions. The decision of who replaces whom in the event of an incumbent vacating that position is nearly always made on the grounds of technical competency.

Again, nonjob attributes are rarely factored into these succession or promotion decisions. Succession planning boils down to finding or grooming an employee who has the same or similar job skills-set. It is often the case that this replacement, selected to succeed the incumbent, is from the same functional area and usually the next level down in the organizational hierarchy. This process for finding a successor is understandable. But this identification process doesn't always consider the totality of the role. More about this in Chapter 15.

Managers during the standard annual or biannual performance review typically confine their appraisals to the technical aspects of the employee's work. The manager's interest is usually whether the jobholder has carried out the literal requirement of the job description. This technical approach to appraising performance is generally promoted by HR. Again, the cost of sticking stringently to the letter of the job description is that vital nonjob behaviors get by-passed or, sometimes, referred to transiently.

This is further complicated by the appraisal process. Countless employees across all industries—even though they don't deserve it—get fair, or even good, evaluation ratings at performance review time. This is often attributable to a lack of attention paid to significant nonjob roles. Many *average* or *above average* employees exhibit substandard, or even appalling, nonjob behavior.

In summary, at the heart of the job description are several KRAs, representing the framework for the successful execution of a job. The employee is recruited and selected based on these KRAs. They are inducted into the organization with these job-related task requirements top-of-mind. The employee is then trained and developed to excel in these job tasks. Further on, succession plans, and promotion opportunities are based on technical nous. The technically competent employee is promoted to leadership positions, even though the new role requires a different set of skills. Pay decisions are substantiated almost exclusively on the task-related components in the job description. We formally assess the employee's performance once or twice a year against these technical KRAs and their associated KPIs. The job description is omnipotent in the employee lifecycle.

And it's also worth repeating that we use the job description to justify sacking someone—it provides legal cover to the manager and company in these circumstances. Although managers use the job description as rationalization for termination of someone's employment, it is, ironically, dreadful nonjob behavior that's the real reason for dismissal. There is no doubting the influence of the job description—it guides and informs every major HR practice the employee is exposed to, ranging from selection to termination.

The pitfalls in the HR practices we have covered in this chapter, resulting from an overreliance of the job description, can be overcome by replacing this outdated work document with a role description.

A role description captures both job and nonjob roles of employees. It's multidimensional. The role description doesn't focus exclusively on the task-specific job requirements. By transitioning from a job to role description, the employer is acknowledging explicitly the totality of the employee's organizational contribution.

Successfully executing a bundle of tasks, we call a job will continue to be important. But the employee should bring more than their technical competence to their employment. Taking on several roles covering both job and nonjob responsibilities is a more realistic reflection of work performance in the 21st century. This is the essence of shifting from a job-focus to a performance-focus.

Where the Rubber Meets the Road

What the Experts Say

When a team member procrastinates or displays a bad attitude, there's a real risk of social contagion that drags down the morale and productivity of those around them. "We all pick up on subtle cues from other people, and that affects our behaviors and actions," says Susan David, founder of the Harvard/McLean Institute of Coaching and author of *Emotional Agility*. "That leads to poor team efficiency, lower levels of commitment, and less focus on the shared goal." Ignoring the issue often ends up only making it more acute. "There are a lot of negative consequences to somebody not carrying his or her load on a team," says Allan Cohen, a professor of management at Babson College and author of *Influence Without Authority*. "The longer it goes on, the worse it gets in terms of how frustrated other members of the group will become." (O'Hara 2017)[2]

Shifting to a role description means that the jobholder is expected to undertake five roles rather than one role—the job role. The other four roles, we covered in the previous chapter are:

- Positive attitude and enthusiasm
- Team role
- Skill development role
- Innovation and continuous improvement role

In practice, this means that the work document be extended to include KPIs and targets for each of these four nonjob roles. This elevated the status of important nonjob performance. Further, by moving to a role description, the HR practices we have discussed will change too. Nonjob performance will be considered in each of the phases of the employee lifecycle. If a focus on performance is two-dimensional, including job and nonjob competencies, the organization can deal more effectively with the changing world of work.

In its execution, shifting to role descriptions should be done collaboratively. There are differences in the types of work and how it's accomplished, not just across industries, but also within organizations. Therefore, consideration needs to be given to how these four nonjob roles are interpreted. Employees should be consulted on how nonjob roles should be applied to the work that they do.

Aside from consulting those whom the role description is designed for, collaboration gives employees buy in. This helps the employee to accept that nonjob roles are important in terms of their own and others' performance. I've done a lot of legwork around KPIs for each of these four nonjob roles in my book, *The End of the Job Description: Shifting from a Job-Focus to a Performance-Focus*.[3] But the main purpose of this chapter is to motivate you to consider a shift from the job description to a role description as an integral part of developing people at work.

Ten Key Takeaways

1. Excelling at a job and performing at work are not necessarily the same.
2. In the quest to find the more technically competent candidate, nonjob attributes are often overlooked.
3. This sends a signal in the starting phase of the employee lifecycle that nonjob roles don't need development.
4. During the induction and onboarding process, there is a strong emphasis on preparing the new employee to undertake their job role. Less emphasis is placed on expectations around nonjob behavior.
5. Training programs that build nonjob competencies, such as team development, are more prevalent than they once were, but less prominent than job competency development.
6. Like the starting and developing, the reward phase of the employee lifecycle sidesteps the development of nonjob skills.
7. As with the other HR practices, the job description has an unhealthy sway on succession planning decisions.
8. Managers during the standard annual or biannual performance review typically confine their appraisals to the technical aspects of the employee's work.

9. Although managers use the job description as rationalization for terminating someone's employment, it is, ironically, dreadful nonjob behavior that's the real reason for dismissal.

10. Shifting to a role description means that the jobholder is expected to undertake five roles rather than one role—the job role.

CHAPTER 13

Shift 8: Job Design to Job Redesign

The modern idea of the job is like a grain of sand on a beach in terms of its historic longevity.

> During our lifetime, most of us spends about 40 years in the workforce, unless we're fortunate enough to win lotto or reap a sizable inheritance. During employment, we devote approximately half our waking hours during the work week on the job. Sadly, most people see this enormous chunk of time as a struggle, or at least, a bore, looking forward to the weekend. For it is on the weekend that these people can then indulge in worthwhile pursuits. That's a big slab of potentially wasted time! (Baker 2021)[1]

In the previous chapter, we looked at shifting from a job description to a role description. The job description is based on a job specification; the conventional framework used for job design. Our job specification system is intended to ensure that the organization is efficient and effective, with a clear delineation between lots of jobs to ensure there aren't gaps or duplication of necessary work.

But job specification's strength is also a liability. The job specification, by design, is rigid and inflexible. A strict and unbending system offers the jobholder a clear sense of what is expected of them. It works effectively in a predictable and stable environment. In an unstable and changeable marketplace, it's a liability.

We don't need to throw out the job specification entirely, however. But job design can be improved significantly by encouraging job crafting. We look at job crafting as a developmental opportunity in this chapter.

Job crafting gives the jobholder an opportunity to redesign their job to suit their strengths and preferences.

Although job crafting isn't a new concept, the post-COVID environment gives HR an opportunity to adopt some fresh thinking about the way work is done. Work can be reshaped to be more adaptable, without discarding job specification. To do this, we need to take a step back. The concept of the job as we know it has only existed for 200-plus years. Before the Industrial Revolution, there was work, of course. But not jobs with a tight job specification, performance regime, and a set of KPIs.

In historical terms, jobs are a recent construct. The modern idea of the job is like a grain of sand on a beach in terms of its historic longevity. Work, without a job design, has been around since the dawn of civilization. It's therefore reasonable to assume the design of the job, as we know it, has been a significant but passing phase. While jobs may disappear, work will not; it never has, and probably never will. Rethinking work, past a series of clearly defined tasks with KPIs, is another necessary mindset shift.

In practice, this means moving from job design to job redesign. This involves promoting job crafting; that is, altering the rigid boundaries of job specification. Like the shift from job descriptions to role descriptions, there's no reason to think of it as an either-or-situation. Job specification and job crafting can coexist. Both approaches can work in tandem.

Job crafting has many benefits and strengths. For starters, job crafting has the potential to offer employees more engagement in their work. And if done well, it means the business is more responsive to the uncertainties of the world we face. Job redesign needs to be less rigidity and more maneuverable.

Understanding Job Specification

By design, current job specification is purposely inflexible; it imposes a strait jacket on the jobholder. It can be risky and career limiting for a jobholder to step outside the bounds of their job specification. But displaying the initiative needed to deal with increasingly complex problems and challenges employees face in their work often requires adaptableness. Job specification was designed after all for a steady and anticipated environment, where controlling the output of the jobholder was economical.

Job specification originated from Taylorism. A job specification breaking down a job into a simple series of predetermined tasks. The job design is assigned to a trained jobholder to perform each task in a preset way. Although the work we do has transformed since the days of the Ford assembly line, the way work is design hasn't fundamentally changed.

There are, nonetheless, several advantages to designing work around a job specification. Breaking tasks into small, easy-to-manage elements, with clearly defined repetitive processes, lessens the skill requirement of the job itself. Job specification lessens the discretionary effort in doing the assigned tasks—including being creative and displaying initiative. This reduces costs. Training is standardized and can be packaged in a procedure's manual. Recurring tasks are broken into simple parts that are easy to learn. Getting people skilled up is quick and cost-effective.

But job specification has its drawbacks, as I mentioned. From a motivational perspective, breaking a job into small, monotonous, and simple parts can make work dull and monotonous. By design, there's little scope for creative thinking and variety. Boredom doing simple, repetitive tasks leads to negative consequences, such as disengagement and absenteeism. Job specification can be ineffectual and even counterproductive in a VUCA world. In a volatile marketplace—which is now the norm—the workforce needs to continually adjust its approach in response to extraordinary conditions.

Successfully producing products and services in a competitive and ever-changing environment now requires agility and ingenuity. This agile response can't be generically documented in a job specification or its buddy, the job description. Job specification puts the onus on the manager to be accountable for making sure people are following the system. This control deprives the jobholder of the ultimate responsibility and ownership of job output.

Although a job specification has served us well as a way of holding the jobholder accountable for their work, it fails to encourage independent judgment. Job specification breeds tunnel vision. The employee cannot understand nor appreciate the way the rest of the organization operates— and doesn't necessarily want or need to. This blinkered thinking is designed to get the employee to focus all their energies on doing a few, manageable work tasks to a predetermined standard.

What Is Job Crafting?

Having considered nonjob roles and their value in the last two chapters, let's now turn our attention to the concept of job crafting as an antedote to the limitations of job specification.

Job crafting is modifying a job to make it more engaging and meaningful for the jobholder. Furthermore, reshaping a job is done by the jobholder, not the manager. The jobholder makes constructive changes to their job, either by how they think about their job, or what they do in their job (Petrou, Demerouti, Peeters, Schaufeli, and Hetland 2012).[2] Three drivers for job crafting are:

- Gaining more control over work.
- Engaging more in the work.
- Developing better connections with others at work.

These motivations lead to a jobholder reshaping their job.

Amy Wrzensniewski, professor of organizational behavior at Yale University, is credited with the concept of job crafting. She and her colleagues studied hospital cleaners job crafting, employees in a manufacturing firm, women working in advocacy nonprofit organizations, and IT workers for the past 20 years. The idea has been slow to take hold.

Job crafting involves taking proactive steps and applying practical actions to remodel the job. Job redesign can be done by changing the tasks, altering the way one interacts with others, or generating fresh perceptions of the work (Berg, Dutton, and Wrzesniewski 2007).[3]

The assumption supporting job crafting is that by changing what's done and the rationale for doing it, the jobholder develops more engagement from the work they do. By redesigning their job, the jobholder potentially gains greater job satisfaction, and the business is more productive and responsive to their market.

With job crafting, there's still a need to do the core functional tasks that are part of the jobholder's responsibility, expressed in their job description. However, this is balanced by expressing the occupant's strengths and interests (Wrzesniewski, Berg, and Dutton 2010).[4] There's evidence that job crafting improves work performance (Caldwell and O'Reilly 1990),[5] boosts motivation, and lifts engagement (Halbesleben, 2010 and

Dubbelt, Demerouti, and Rispens 2019).[6] Job crafting can unleash the enterprising qualities of the individual. This is a hopeful and refreshing departure from the imposed shackles of job specification.

Let's briefly consider the three ways to job craft.

The most obvious approach, referred to as *task crafting*, involves adding or eliminating certain activities, modifying the time or amount of effort spent on various job duties, or redesigning aspects of a given task. The second method, referred to as *relational crafting*, includes creating, maintaining, modifying, or eliminating relationships with others at work. And the third approach, called *cognitive crafting*, entails reframing the perception and interpretation of the job's purpose. Let's look at each approach in more detail.

Task Crafting

Task crafting is adjusting the ways certain tasks are performed or taking on more or fewer tasks. Of the three forms of job crafting, task crafting is the most tangible approach. Because it impacts the job specification directly, it's the most noticeable form of job crafting. The other two approaches indirectly affect the job.

With task crafting, the jobholder is essentially shaping or molding their work role to accommodate their strengths by adjusting the tasks they do, or not do. This can mean adding, dropping, or modifying the KRAs in the job description. The job tasks are redesigned to better suit the person in the role, in other words.

Consider this simple illustration of task crafting.

Harry, a bus driver, decides to give helpful sightseeing advice while traveling his regular route from the airport to the city. He's mindful that many of his passengers are from out of town. Harry perceives his job as more than driving a bus (cognitive crafting). By using his extensive local knowledge, Harry decides to use his extroverted personality to good effect. He decides to add sightseeing to his primary task of driving a bus.

The jobholder (Harry) elects to take on an additional task beyond their original job specification. Harry added this task because he enjoyed doing it and it played to his strength. What's more, he saw his job as more than a bus driver, which entails another approach: cognitive crafting.

Adding tasks is one way to task craft, but there are other ways too. Task crafting can include changing the nature of certain responsibilities or taking away tasks. It might also involve dedicating a different proportion of time to certain tasks or devoting time to certain projects. These changes needn't affect the focus of job the occupant is hired to do.

Relational Crafting

Relational crafting focuses on changing the jobholder's interactions with others in carrying out their work. These working relationships, either within or beyond the workplace, are formed or reframed for better impact. This type of crafting emphasizes how people can restructure the way they deal with others to achieve their KPIs, in other words.

Relational crafting entails changing *who* the jobholder works with on different tasks and projects or *how* they communicate and engage stakeholders. For instance, the employee can relationally craft by interacting with different departments they have neglected previously (who). Or they can make certain projects collaborative exercises that were done autonomously in the past (how).

Tom is a salesperson who sells digital solutions. He seeks out Marco, the firm's app designer in another department, to discuss making the user interface simpler for his customers. Although not a stakeholder, Tom's several interactions with Marco are fruitful and leads a more accessible menu that improves the company's product. With his understanding of his customer's needs, particularly their limited digital literacy, Tom shares his firsthand knowledge with Marco to improve the menu interface.

In this case, the jobholder (Tom) preemptively seeks out others and this leads to changing their perspective and others to produce a better solution for the customer.

Cognitive Crafting

Cognitive crafting is changing the way the jobholder thinks about their work. Furthermore, this approach refashioning the way one thinks about their job's impact on others. While the first two approaches to job crafting change the actions people take, this method involves choosing to reframe the jobholder's mindset about what they do at work. With a change of perspective on the purpose of their job, the jobholder can find or create more meaning. Without a sense of purpose, work is often dull and unfulfilling.

Jon is a policy officer in a government agency. Policy officers are responsible for churning out endless policy papers. Jon doesn't think of it that way. He chooses to view this work as a valuable contribution to building a better society. Jon feels that the work he does can guide and inform good public policy for the benefit of his country.

An employee adopting this type of crafting thinks constructively about their job and how it contributes to a greater purpose beyond going through the motions.

Where the Rubber Meets the Road

A Greater Sense of Meaning in Her Job

Candice Walker is a housekeeper at a university hospital. Her primary interest has always been the patients the organization serves and their families. From the time she started her job, she saw her work as much more than her cleaning responsibilities. Instead, she cognitively reframed her work as a form of healing, playing a key role "in the house of hope." Defining her role as healer meant she paid additional attention to the tasks that might help people recover and leave the hospital more quickly. This meant dedicating extra care to cleaning bathroom features during the winter season so her patients weren't endangered. It also meant anticipating and providing materials that might be in short supply so that the patient could feel "things were in their control" and that they were moving toward a faster release to home. She also formed relationships with patients and their families, getting to know them as people, not just temporary patients.

Candice used her emotional intelligence to make gentle inquiries that showed care and interest, without overstepping boundaries. She used similar skills to decide who might need additional attention and conversation on a particular day or night because they were experiencing pain, fear, or loneliness. She would then alter which patients she spent time with so that her work could make a bigger difference in their lives. By cognitively crafting her job in these ways, Candice reported finding a greater sense of meaning in her job. (Dutton and Wrzesniewski 2020)[7]

Job crafting—whether it's task, relational, or cognitive—requires positive proactive behavior from the employee. This can enable more meaning from work. Although job crafting is employee initiated, managers need to support it by creating the right environment. With management encouragement, positive changes become an effective and sustainable form of enterprising behavior. The three types of job crafting—with their different emphases—are not mutually exclusive, however. Job crafters may exercise any combination of the three dimensions.

Using any of the three approaches, or a combination, the employee can redesign their work to capitalize on their strengths and interests. The employee, in other words, with the support of their manager, can change their job to be more meaningful and productive. To be clear: Job crafting is not completely abandoning important tasks and doing whatever comes to mind.

Since job crafting is an employee-driven initiative, what's HRs role? HR can create a receptive environment for job crafting to prosper. This would include training on job crafting and orchestrating collaborative meetings between leaders and their teams to facilitate a more flexible interpretation of the current job design. Success stories can be shared. You can find more detail of a job crafting program in my book, *Breaking the Proactive Paradox: Maximizing Empowerment Through Empowerment*.[8]

In the next chapter, we consider the development of the super team and how AI and humans can collaborate.

Ten Key Takeaways

1. The job specification, by design, is rigid and inflexible.
2. In historical terms, jobs are a recent construct.
3. Job specification and job crafting can coexist. Both approaches can work in tandem.
4. Job crafting has the potential to offer employees more engagement in their work.
5. By design, current job specification is purposely inflexible; it imposes a strait jacket on the jobholder.
6. A job specification breaking down a job into a simple series of predetermined tasks.

7. Job crafting is modifying a job to make it more engaging and meaningful for the jobholder.
8. Task crafting is adjusting the ways certain tasks are performed or taking on more or fewer tasks.
9. Relational crafting focuses on changing the jobholder's interactions with others in carrying out their work.
10. Cognitive crafting is changing the way the jobholder thinks about their work.

CHAPTER 14

Shift 9: Competition to Partnership

We can't stem the tide of technology any more than we can stem the tide of the oceans. But we can be smarter about how we collaborate with it.

The idea of the super team builds on two changes over the past decade. One development is the rise of teams and its prominence in the organizing structure of companies. And the other development is the adoption of AI in the workplace.

With flatter hierarchical structures and the digitalization of the workplace, pressure is placed on organizations to redesign themselves. Speed, agility, and adaptability are now the drivers of business success. These imperatives resulted in decentralized decisions gravitating to teams. Most businesses attest to more flexibility and better performance through teams.

The emerging idea that machines shouldn't be seen as a competitor for human jobs turns the focus to humans and AI collaborating. AI is now viewed as an enabler to help humans do their job better and to be more effective in their work practices. This shift from competition to collaboration has been an uncomfortable transition for many organizations, and still is, to some extent. HR has a role in easing this discomfort. For starters, jobs can be designed to accommodate tasks being done more successfully through automation. Time can be freed up for people to do what they can do best, such as dealing empathetically with difficult customers.

The rise of teams and the adoption of AI come together to create the concept of the super team. The evolving idea is that by putting AI into team activity, organizations and individuals can reinvent themselves, work together in new, more productive ways. (Deloitte Global Human Capital Trends 2020)[1]

In the previous chapter we looked at improving job specification, the system used for the past 100 years to structure work in organizations. This development can be done by actively encouraging job crafting. In this final chapter on the developing phase of the employee lifecycle, we'll look at shifting from competition between humans and AI to collaboration.

AI, as we discussed in Chapter 2, is getting better and better at doing more and more human tasks. Technology can diagnose diseases, translate languages, provide customer service, and a whole host of other functions. Not only can AI accomplish these traditional human responsibilities, but it can also now do them more efficiently and effectively.

You might recall that Professor David Susskind, the eminent Oxford economist, canvasses the possibility of a world without work. We can't of course know whether this will eventuate. But if it does happen, Susskind concedes that it's not going to happen within the next decade. Whether he's right or wrong in his claim, I suggest we plan for the short and medium terms. We need to accept the inevitable: AI is and will continue to be an ally in helping employees (and their employers) be more successful, at least in the short term. We can't stem the tide of technology any more than we can stem the tide of the oceans. But we can be smarter about how we collaborate with it.

AI continues to radically alter how work is done, and who does it. At least for now—before the sobering possibility of a jobless world—the immediate impact of technology will be in complementing human capability, not replacing it. Companies are achieving significant performance improvements when humans and machines work together.[2] James Wilson and Paul Daugherty of Accenture, explain this new mindset:

> Through such collaborative intelligence, humans and AI actively enhance each other's complementary strengths: the leadership, teamwork, creativity, and social skills of the former, and the speed, scalability, and quantitative capacities of the latter. What comes naturally to people (making a joke, for example) can be tricky for machines, and what straightforward for machines (analyzing gigabytes of data) remains virtually impossible for humans.[3]

Businesses need humans and technology to prosper.

To work collaboratively, an understanding and appreciation of the strengths and weaknesses of humans and machines is the starting point. How can machines enhance the work of employees? What do humans now do better than machines? Teams can then allocate work responsibilities based on the answers to these two questions. Machines and people then become a partnership that Wilson and Daugherty call *collaborative intelligence.*

Broadly, is response to the first question, there are three ways smart machines can contribute to the team. First, AI can amplify employees' cognitive strengths. Machines can crunch masses of data to validate a solution to solving typical customer problems, for instance. Second, AI is useful to deal with low level customer questions and inquiries. This frees up the team member to be concentrating on high-level tasks. And third, machines can extend employees' physical capacities to get more do in less time, such as identifying defects in the mass production of items.[4]

Where the Rubber Meets the Road

Aida Comes to the Rescue

SBE, a major Swedish bank, now uses a virtual assistant called Aida to interact with millions of customers. Able to handle natural language conversations, Aida has access to vast stores of data and can answer many frequently asked questions, such as how I open an account or make cross border payments. "She" can also ask callers follow up questions to solve their problems, and she's able to analyze a caller's tone of voice (frustrated versus appreciative, for instance) and use that information to provide better service later. Whenever the system can't resolve an issue—which happens in about 30 percent of cases—it turns the caller over to a human customer service representative and then monitors that interaction to learn how to resolve similar problems in the future. With Aida handling basic requests, humans can concentrate on addressing more complex issues, especially those from unhappy callers then might require extra handholding. (HBR's 10 Must Reads Series 2019)[5]

The Rise of AI and Organizational Readiness

AI is projected to add U.S. $13 trillion to global economy over the next decade (Fountaine, McCarthy, and Saleh 2019).[6] Even so, many firms may not be prepared for this. According to the 2020 Deloitte global human capital trends report, 59 percent say that redesigning jobs to integrate AI technology is important or very important for their success over the next 12 to 18 months. However, only 7 percent say that they are very ready to address this trend (Deloitte Global Human Capital Trends 2020).[7]

For decades, predictions have been grim, with headlines playing seemingly endless variations on "robots are coming for your job." That's a lot of threatening and negative conditioning. We are now starting to accept that cutting costs by eliminating human jobs isn't the only path available for AI. As the 2020 Deloitte's report states, "organizations face a fundamental choice: whether to use AI solely to automate tasks formally performed by people, or to use it to assist workers as well."[8] In other words, should AI be used to increase consistency and productivity or add value to what humans are doing?

Currently, only 16 percent of organizations are using AI primarily to assist employees to develop insights (Deloitte Global Human Capital Trends 2020).[9] The remaining 84 percent of organizations are presumedly using AI to improve consistency in quality and increasing productivity. So, we have some way to go in changing the mindset from competition to collaboration.

Using machines to displace workers through automation is misguided and shortsighted. This conventional approach isn't yielding the full potential of AI. Progressive businesses are adopting a different mindset. They are shifting from the idea of competition between humans and machines for jobs to employees and technology collaborating to produce super jobs is the way of the future. By embracing this mentality, companies can transform their operations, their customer experience, and their workforces.

The big challenge for most businesses is to think differently about AI and how it can be utilized. What's more, the mentality should be to transform work and jobs in ways that generate value. This requires companies to consider ways of integrating AI into teamwork. Teams, as we know, are the fundamental building block where most work is accomplished in today's workplaces. The challenge is to find ways to thoroughly assimilate AI into workplace teams.

Even before considering this, some companies are still stuck in the past in the way they structure their workplaces, emphasizing hierarchy and the chain-of-command. But we are evolving from functional-based work structures to project-based teams. You'll recall that this was one of the eight shifts in beliefs transitioning from the old to the new employment relationship we discussed in Chapter 9. But from personal experience as a consultant, many firms find it hard to let go of their old org chart, with a series of boxes reporting to one another. You'd hope that after 100 years of bureaucratic hierarchies, we'd be ready to move on.

Super Jobs to Super Teams

The concept of the "super job" is discussed by management consultant, Erica Vollini, and colleagues, in the article, *From Jobs to Superjobs*.[10] Super jobs are jobs that combine work and responsibilities with technology to broaden the scope of the work performed. These super jobs combine what humans and machines do best to magnify the productive impact of work.

Super teams are an extension of this idea. These teams combine people and machines to leverage their collective capabilities to solve problems, gain insights, and create value. Thomas Malone of MIT has been exploring how groups of humans and machines can work together to achieve new levels of intelligence. As I mentioned earlier, this is that Wilson and Daugherty of Accenture refer to as collaborative intelligence.[11]

One of the more obvious examples of collaboration in super teams is how rudimentary work is done. It's inevitable that human involvement in basic tasks that need to be done accurately and efficiency will continue to be done by smart machines. This frees up people to make better decisions faster.

It's inevitable that this evolution from a job to team focus is the next frontier. Augmenting humans in teams with technology to form super teams is on the horizon.

Let's take stock.

There's a logical progression in play. Stage one was—and in many cases still is—replacing people with technology to reduce costs and improve efficiency. Stage two is the augmentation of technology and people to drive greater value and expand business opportunities. This is the stage where most businesses are in. In this phase, there's still a mentality that machines can reduce employment costs and improve efficiency. The next stage we are entering is collaborative intelligence. And within this phase, we are progressing from super jobs to super teams. This stage, once fully embraced by industry, involves work done in super teams, where machines and humans work together to produce greater results. To arrive at this third stage, mindsets need to change, jobs need to be restructured, and new training and development opportunities need to be provided.

As I said in Chapter 10, from an L&D perspective, we need to emphasis the person- and problem-centered dimensions of learning. Critical thinking, conflict resolution, teamwork, and collaboration all play a role in the super team structure. This new structure also requires a different type of leadership.

It's now obvious that moving toward the concept of super teams will require more investment in person-centered and problem-centered learning. Also from a developmental perspective, shifting from job to role descriptions (Chapter 12) is necessary too. It's apparent that the four nonjob roles (positive attitude and enthusiasm, team, skill development, and innovation and continuous improvement) I outlined (and others) will gain more prominence in the collaboration between people and intelligent machines.

The choice is clear for business, as Volini states:

> Organizations that continue to manage AI and humans on parallel tracks will continue to be able to make moderate gains in efficiency, while organizations that choose to integrate humans and AI into super teams can realize much greater value by redesigning work in transformative ways. (Deloitte Global Human Capital Trends 2020)[12]

What specifically is the role of humans in super teams? Humans needs to *train*, *explain*, and *sustain* (HBR's 10 Must Reads Series 2019).[13] Training machines to perform certain tasks is part of the fourth dimension of L&D: machine-centered learning. Apart from job-centered, person-centered, and problem-centered, we can add machine-centered learning, as I suggest in Chapter 12. Specialists with the necessary knowledge and skills-set working with AI, will be in increasing demand. These specialists will have to train other humans too.

Experts also need to be able to interpret and explain the outcomes of the work of machines when the data is inconclusive or controversial. As we become more and more reliant on machines, there will be a greater array of responses that need to be deciphered and communicated to practitioners within the team. These practitioners will rely on these data to make decisions. For instance, in evidence-based industries, such as medicine, the physician must understand how AI arrived at its conclusions and recommendations.

Sustaining the machines is the third role. In addition to having people who can explain AI outcomes, members of the super team need to continually ensure that AI systems are working properly, safety, and ethically. All three roles are dependent on machine-centered L&D.

In turn, machines' role in super teams can improve performance in several ways. AI can improve business processes to:

- Be more agile;
- Increase production speed;
- Enhance the scale and scope of activity; and
- Make better decisions and to provide personalized solutions for customers.

All these ways capitalize on the strengths of AI and mitigate the limitations of humans.

In the introduction of this book, I discussed the Ford Motor Company and the formation of its assembly lines, using the principles of scientific management. It's ironic that over 100 years later, at the height of the pandemic, Ford was applying the principles of super teams. Through collaborative intelligence, the company was able to use their specialized teams to set up new product lines in its manufacturing facilities. These teams then pivoted from making hybrid car batteries to manufacture thousands of ventilators.

From a HR perspective, perhaps the greatest value the concept of the super team promises is its vast potential to transform the nature of work, at least in the short-to-medium term. By fully harnessing technology and its infinite capacities, it frees up the employee to do what humans (still) do best. Human traits such as:

- Creative problem solving;
- Their capacity to surpass expectations (machines can do no better yet than to meet expectations);
- Build bonds; and
- Show empathy

can be optimized. By using technology to design work in ways that allow humans to perform at their best, organizational work is transformed.

This can mean working collaboratively in teams, breaking down silos to work cross-functionally, creating knowledge, learning on the job, and humanizing the work experience.

This brings us to the end of PART 3. We now move to the rewarding phase of the employee lifecycle, beginning with how we need to shift our thinking about the way we promote people into leadership roles.

Ten Key Takeaways

1. AI is getting better and better at doing more and more human tasks.
2. To work collaboratively, an understanding and appreciation of the strengths and weaknesses of humans and machines is the starting point.
3. AI is projected to add U.S. $13 trillion to global economy over the next decade.
4. Using machines to displace workers through automation is misguided and shortsighted.
5. Super teams combine people and machines to leverage their collective capabilities to solve problems, gain insights, and create value.
6. One of the more obvious examples of collaboration in super teams is how rudimentary work is done.

7. For super teams to work mindsets need to change, jobs need to be restructured, and new training and development opportunities need to be provided.

8. It's now obvious that moving toward the concept of super teams will require more investment in person-centered and problem-centered learning.

9. The role of humans in super teams is to train, explain, and sustain.

10. Machines' role in super teams can improve performance in several ways.

PART 4

Rewarding Phase
of Employment

CHAPTER 15

Shift 10: Technical Knowhow to People Leadership

A leader needs to motivate, communicate, influence, delegate, and coordinate. Why then do we promote people to leadership posts primarily on their technical knowhow?

The investors and board of PLC expect an elevated level of foresight by its executive team. "We need to have succession plans that are for the next 12 or 24 months or an even longer timeframe than that," says Sarah Totham, Director of Talent and Organisational Development.

The FTSE 100 financial services company is organized into seven divisions, including investment management, insurance, and mature savings. Each one is headed by a divisional CEO reporting into the group CEO, Nigel Wilson. One of the key challenges in such organizations is moving talent between divisions. But, of course, it is also an opportunity.

"We have moved people around a lot. The internal appointments of divisional CEOs have all moved from one part of the business to head up a different business," says Totham.

"Next level down, we work with the divisional CEOs on the development plans for their teams so encouraging moves across the group because these CEOs tend to work within their verticals." (Welsh 2019)[1]

This is the first chapter of PART 4—the rewarding phase of employment. In this part of the employee lifecycle, we consider three issues: succession planning and the pearls of promoting technicians to leadership roles; our fixation with appraising rather than developing employees; and persisting with extrinsic motivators when we should be emphasizing intrinsic motivation. These three mindset shifts affect the rewarding phase of employment. This chapter considers the shift from technical leadership to people leadership.

Succession planning is the practice of identifying and developing people with the potential to fill key leadership positions in the future. Unfortunately, as I stated in my recent book, *Breaking the Proactive Paradox: Maximizing Performance Through Empowerment,*[2] there is more emphasis on identifying successors rather than preparing them for their next role. Yet again, the job description has too much sway in succession planning, as it does in all HR practices for rewarding employees. Put simply, plugging a gap in the org chart is mostly decided on technical competence. Nontechnical qualities are generally overlooked, or at least, not given the same consideration.

Succession planning's standard practice is recognizing someone with a similar technical skill set to the incumbent. What's more, the replacement is usually selected from the same functional area and the next level down in the organizational hierarchy. This appears a sensible practice but can be problematic for moving from a technical to leadership role.

To prepare the successor for the eventual promotion, their training needs are analyzed. This assessment is based mostly on the technical requirements of the following job. Although technical competence must be considered, nontechnical deficiencies are frequently overlooked. The successor's training and development plan is predominantly task-related, in other words. At best, development opportunities outside the scope of the job description are given lesser priority.

Let me illustrate my point. Joanne has been identified and groomed as Mary's replacement. Mary is the senior finance officer for a large firm. The position involves extensive informal contact with several *difficult* stakeholders. As an internal service provider, Mary currently deals with many people on a variety of financial matters. Although this isn't cited in the position's job specification. Dealing effectively with people in other departments is crucial for success in Mary's role. But this vital feature of the role isn't covered in Joanna's training plan. Joanna's succession training emphasizes the technical requirements of Mary's role. But success in her new role is largely dependent on building constructive working relationships with many people across the company. Not including this nontechnical aspect in Joanna's succession plan means she is ill prepared for the role.

Succession planning for leadership roles is often poorly done. Making the transition from a technical to a leadership role involves a fundamentally different skill set. The two roles are poles apart. For starters, the technical role is task-related, and the leadership role is people-related. The technical position involves doing the work, which entails a command of procedural knowledge, whereas the leadership position is overseeing the technical work done by others. A leader needs to motivate, communicate, influence, delegate, and coordinate. Why then do we promote people to leadership posts primarily on their technical knowhow?

The answer: A dependency on the task-specific job description to make promotional decisions.

It's nonsensical to promote people to leadership roles because they have great technical qualifications and skills. There are Dilbert-style jokes about this practice. Just because someone is a terrific engineer, for instance, doesn't necessarily mean they will be a terrific leader of engineers. The skill sets aren't transferrable. A leader's knowledge of the intimate details of technical tasks—although undoubtedly useful—is less relevant than their ability to lead people to do the tasks. This all-too-familiar practice of promoting skilled technicians to managerial roles is another reason to rethink job design.

This isn't only a problem for internal promotions. When recruiting externally to fill a leadership role, the selection decision is still based mainly on technical competence and experience. The first step in the selection process—even for roles that predominantly involve managing and leading—is to find candidates who match the functional criterion. If a candidate ticks all the technical boxes, the assumption is that they are "qualified" to lead others in that discipline. With too much emphasis on technical knowledge and experience, succession planning and promotion is obstructed by the way we currently design and document jobs.

Across all industries, technical experts who perform well eventually get promoted into leading a team to deliver results through the team. The conventional pathway to advancing in one's career is typically by moving into management, even if one is ill equipped to be a leader of people. Unfortunately, if the candidate for promotion don't learn these new skills, they are likely to end up underperforming.

Let me illustrate what I mean. One of my recent coaching clients is Jacob. Jacob is head of engineering in a large civil engineering consulting firm. At one of our coaching sessions, he was at his wits end. Jacob was six months into his new role as manager. During that time, he identified opportunities to increase efficiency and transparency and develop a strategy and path for implementing changes. But he had an interpersonal conflict with Marianne. He shared his frustrations with me. Jacob was not on the same page as Marianne, one of his key team members. He complained to me in the coaching session that he believed he clearly explained the changes he wanted to Marianne and what she needed to do to implement those changes. However, Marianne ignored his suggestions and continued to run things the same way. This frustration consumed Jacob's time and energy and held back the rollout of his strategy.

Jacob has 15 years of relevant experience and had a sharp analytical mind; he was well qualified to identify these changes he wanted to implement. But his mastery of solving technical challenges contrasted sharply with his inability to influence his team members. Jacob is no different from hundreds of other leaders I've coached. Jacob's plight illustrates an underlying problem that I've observed over 20 years of coaching and training leaders promoted for their technical competence.

People get promoted regularly across all industries into leadership roles because of technical or functional skills and expertise that enable them to perform well in their technical domain. But that doesn't translate into effective leadership. Many of these new leaders struggle to inspire, coach, influence, and build commitment to a shared vision. They are self-disciplined and focused on doing their job as a technical expert. Transitioning into a leadership role, however, requires cultivating ownership and accountability in their team.

Many companies fall short in filling the gap with the training and coaching necessary to develop technical or functional experts into skilled leaders. Unfortunately, they failed to prioritize effective leadership in their reward systems and culture. Without clearly articulating what effective leadership looks like in practice, valuing it, and providing structured opportunities to get better at it, they fail to bridge the gap between technical leadership and people leadership.

It's therefore unsurprising that new (and even experienced) managers often operate under misguided assumptions about leadership. What's more, the leader doesn't understand and appreciate their own contribution to the people issues in their new team. They misdiagnose these situations and try to solve it with a technical solution, ignoring the people dimension until it becomes a performance management drama. As Monique Valcour, executive coach, and management professor, eloquently puts it: "leadership challenges are fundamentally interpersonal in nature; thus, their solutions are as well" (Valcour 2021).[3]

From my experience, one of the factors that separate people who lead from those who simply occupy leadership positions is a desire to embrace continuous learning and growth. The best leaders I know—the same one's you know—make it a practice to self-reflect; they assume that they always have more to learn; and seek and welcome feedback as a learning opportunity.

Making the transition from finding technical solutions to being an expert in leading others isn't easy. Companies must therefore do a better job at supporting this shift. Succession planning and talent development go together. Talent development should equip potential managers with two essential personal perspectives: internal and external.

The internal perspective is the capabilities to look within—to gain self-knowledge and personal insight. Beyond a better understanding of self, the external perspective is to see themselves as part of a system of relationships. Leadership is fundamentally about influencing, communicating, and collaborating with others to affect desirable change. Talent development programs need to be better at preparing people for succession to leadership positions.

The costs of poor succession placements are significant. For example, the amount of market value wiped out by badly managed CEO and C-suite transitions in the S&P 1500 is close to $1 trillion a year (Fernandez, Nagel, and Green 2021).[5] One can only imagine what the dollar figure would be for failed leadership placements in all management positions across all industries. It's a costly exercise not to do leadership succession

---

Where the Rubber Meets the Road

People, Place, and Performance at Unilever

Unilever's HR vision is *People, Place and Performance*, according to Leena Nair, senior vice president of Leadership and Organization Development. She elaborates:

"We have spent an enormous amount of time examining whether we have the talent engine to sustain an 80-billion-euro revenue business. There is a significant amount of talent analytics done around the kinds of people we have, the quality, where the gaps are, how we're going to close the gap, etc. We track and see how we are doing across all these areas. We examine the skills, talent, and culture to see if we have what it takes to be the 80-billion-euro business we want to be. This is one of the essential roles HR plays in the business by ensuring any gaps in the skills, talent or culture across the business that might harm our 80-billion-euro aspirations are covered. It's all about three years from now; five years from now. We are future-proofing the business." (CIPD 2020)[4]

---

planning properly, not just for the company, but the economy too. On the flip side, doing it right can be a huge competitive advantage.

A common dilemma for companies is whether to hire managers internally or externally. Both options have an upside and downside. Hiring externally, particularly for senior roles, is risky. Companies often choose outsiders because they've already served in similar roles elsewhere. This is done because the perceived track record looks attractive against an internal leadership appointment. But that experience rarely translates into success in the new role (Fernandez, Nagel, and Green 2021).[6] Filling a leadership vacancy externally can often be an irrational decision. This can be based on a false belief that a candidate with a perceived unblemished record is exciting, even though the hiring company knows little about the manager.

This isn't an argument for not hiring externally. It's merely a warning that it can be a dicey proposition. If the senior manager is required to transform the culture of the company, an outside appointment can often be a sensible decision. Nevertheless, if a business has a thorough talent development program in place, it can provide the company with more options.

But there are reasons why some of the world's biggest and most powerful organizations get the senior management appointment wrong. Two main reasons are a lack of attention to succession planning and substandard leadership and internal talent development (Fernandez, Nagel, and Green 2021).[7]

As we discussed in Chapter 6, past experience isn't always an accurate indicator of future performance. Good leadership is based on attributes such as curiosity, insight, engagement, and determination. People who demonstrate these capabilities should be identified and groomed for high level positions. We know that emotional intelligence can be developed. Being flexible, adaptable, having self-control, and being able to develop relationships are other traits that can be nurtured.

Succession planning needs to take these factors into account. They aren't the only traits of leadership, and they don't guarantee success transitioning from technical leadership to management. But they are a good starting point.

According to Sara Canaday, a leadership expert and author, technological advancement exacerbates the problem of transitioning from a technical to leadership role.

> While some tech experts prefer to continue as strong individual contributors or follow the domain expertise path, others will be recognized for their outstanding value and be promoted into management.[8]

Companies are understandably rapidly relying more and more on technology experts. Canady claims, however, that this reinforces the misguided belief that technical leaders are capable of being promoted into people leadership positions because of their superior technical knowledge.

Undoubtedly, an integrated strategy that combines succession planning with leadership development can give a company a competitive edge. This strategy helps to buffer the business in turbulent times of uncertainty. This integrated strategy builds the leadership pipeline that is lacking in so many companies worldwide. It also makes promoting from technical leadership to people leadership a more seamless process.

Ten Key Takeaways

1. Succession planning is the practice of identifying and developing people with the potential to fill key leadership positions in the future.
2. Succession planning's standard practice is recognizing someone with a similar technical skill set to the incumbent.
3. It's nonsensical to promote people to leadership roles because they have great technical qualifications and skills.
4. Across all industries, technical experts who perform well eventually get promoted into leading a team to deliver results through the team.
5. Many companies fall short in filling the gap with the training and coaching necessary to develop technical or functional experts into skilled leaders.
6. It's therefore unsurprising that new (and even experienced) managers often operate under misguided assumptions about leadership.
7. The costs of poor succession placements are significant.
8. A common dilemma for companies is whether to hire managers internally or externally.
9. Good leadership is based on attributes such as curiosity, insight, engagement, and determination.
10. Technological advancement exacerbates the problem of transitioning from a technical to leadership role.

CHAPTER 16

Shift 11: Appraising to Developing Performance

How do we make employees more accountable for their performance? This is a perennial challenge that's not helped by an archaic performance management system.

> A unique relationship develops between the manager and employee who regularly enter dialog, as they develop a deeper level of trust. This carries over to task-based discussions in the team. They develop a richer understanding of the uniqueness of each person's point-of-view and experience. Larger understandings emerge by holding one's own perspective "gently." Part of the vision of dialog is the assumption of a "larger pool of meaning" that's accessible to the team. (Senge 2006)[1]

In this chapter, we look at the need to shift from appraising to developing performance. Many companies are taking tentative steps in this direction since the performance review fell out of favor. If you are yet to be persuaded to move to replacing the performance review, I want to reinforce the pitfalls of the performance review. I also want to emphasize the benefits of ongoing developmental conversations between the manager and employee. Good leadership is based on building positive working relationships with team members. Work performance is a joint responsibility between the manager and employee. I'll also share one conversation framework that is gaining traction around the world.

We are seeing changes in the practices of performance management. The annual performance appraisal process has been deeply ingrained in organizations for decades. We are now starting to shift to more frequent development and performance conversations between managers and employees. Although a positive step, I see many companies still too slow in making this move.

I've never been a supporter of the performance review. I wrote *The End of the Performance Review: A New Approach to Appraising Employee Performance* in 2013.[2] In this book, I advocate getting rid of the performance review and replacing it with a new framework. I'll briefly explain the *Five Conversations Framework* later.

The Case Against the Performance Review

First, let me state the case for removing the performance review. If you've replaced the performance review then I say, congratulations. I think you're moving in the right direction. There are, however, many companies who are resisting letting go of this artifact of the 20th century. So, I feel compelled to put the case against the performance review.

Performance appraisals typically come around once or twice a year and they are usually not something that everyone looks forward to. I have spoken to lots of people across many industries over the past decade. And most people aren't enthusiastic about the traditional appraisal interview. Some dread them.

Whether you coordinate the appraisal system, a manager who conducts the appraisals, or an employee on the receiving end of it (or all three), you probably have some reservations about the standardized process. Why? Is it the formality of the process? Is it the paperwork? Is it the unexpected or unknown? Is it the apprehension of what it means for remuneration? Is it the prospects of giving or receiving criticism? It could be all these things and more.

To be fair, not everyone faces the performance appraisal interview with trepidation. Some enjoy it and even look forward to it. But they are in the minority. Most people find the whole experience unproductive and unrewarding. The idea of preparing to appraise someone's work performance or being on the receiving end of an appraisal is not everyone's idea of fun. If that's the experience of most people, we must ask: *Is it worth it?*

The traditional performance appraisal system is based on the military model. Like many things in the military, the performance appraisal has been adopted in the corporate world. In the military environment, the superior gives the subordinate a one-way monolog on what they are doing wrong and occasionally what the subordinate is doing right. The recipient is usually a passive and unenthusiastic receiver of this appraisal. This model is based on a power relationship.

What the boss thinks, irrespective of whether they are right or wrong, carries greater weight than the recipient. The appraiser has power over the person being appraised. Managers control the process and the subordinate dances to the tune of the appraiser. It isn't a constructive dynamic for discussing developmental and performance issues. Like most things military, the performance appraisal system has been modified for industry to some extent but doesn't go far enough to alleviate the power imbalance.

For instance, the power disparity has been somewhat equalized in the civilian (and military) workplace. Employees are now asked to rate themselves and discuss their own perspectives about their performance across several criteria. Good managers try not to do too much talking. They aim to do no more than 50 percent of the talking. Using open-ended questions, the employee is encouraged to contribute.

Irrespective of the manager's interpersonal skills, these meetings are still controlled by the manager. Their opinion generally carries more weight. The conversation is often dominated by the observations the manager has of the employee. So, there is still an imbalance in power. This power dynamic is based on the potentially flawed assumption that managers know best: sometimes they do and sometimes they don't.

There are several inherent problems with this conventional appraisal system. I know this after interviewing 1,200 managers and HR professionals across 21 industries. I simply asked them to identify any shortcomings the standard performance appraisal system has. Responses varied, but essentially, I identified eight themes from my research. The eight shortcomings are that they are:

- Costly
- Potentially destructive
- Often a monolog rather than a dialog
- Too formal and stifle discussion
- Too infrequent
- An exercise in form filing

- Rarely followed up
- Unnecessarily stressful (Baker 2013)[3]

Leadership Is a Relationship

The performance review was designed to achieve two purposes. One purpose is to justify salary decisions. The second purpose is to increase performance. Both purposes are sound. However, using the performance review to achieve both objectives is a difficult balancing act. Reward an employee via a pay rise and motivating higher performance in one meeting is a big ask. Having an annual discussion with an employee about salary can still be achieved without the performance review. And I have yet to see any research that shows that performance reviews increase performance.

"Leadership is a relationship," according to Jim Kouzes and Barry Posner in their book, *Credibility: How Leaders Gain and Lose It.*[4] I think this eloquently sums up the essence of good leadership. Leadership is not a position; it's an aspiration. Leaders must earn the right to lead every day. People choose whether they're going to follow the leader. It's transactional. As Kouzes and Posner state, "leadership is a relationship between those who aspire to lead and those who choose to follow." As we discussed in Chapter 9, changing the employment relationship dynamic from "them & us" to a collaborative working relationship is achieved through regular dialog.

A healthy working relationship—or any relationship—is based on a shared set of expectations. The expectations of the new employment relationship are diametrically opposite to the traditional employment relationship. So, the shift from the them and us relationship to the collaborative partnership is pivotal to the shift from appraising to developing performance.

This is, however, a chicken and the egg situation. Is engaging in regular developmental conversations what changes the employment relationship? Or is a new employment relationship foundational for developmental dialog to take place? I think it's both. But I've no doubt that you can develop a collaborative working relationship through frequent dialog. Likewise, persevering with the annual performance review reinforces the traditional relationship.

Collaborative leaders understand the value of regular catch-ups with their team members. These nontask specific meetings may occur fortnightly or monthly. But they occur, regardless of how busy the manager is—they make it a priority. Alas, as I said earlier, good leaders are in short supply.

I've discovered from experience that suggesting to leaders (even when they agree with me) that they should be having regular catch-ups with their team members isn't sufficient. Business inevitably gets in the way of these catch-ups. So, I think it's important that HR has a proactive role in providing a framework for their leaders to have regular developmental and performance conversations. This puts some gentle pressure on leaders and team members to have routine development and performance conversations.

Accountability

How do we make employees more accountable for their performance? This is a perennial challenge that's not helped by an archaic performance management system. With performance reviews, where the manager controls the process and gives a rating to the employee, all accountability is left with the manager. What we need is for the employee to be more accountable for their own performance. This accountability must tap into the employee's intrinsic motivation that we'll cover in the next chapter.

Managers struggle with this issue of performance accountability. For example, 82 percent of managers in a study admitted that they have "limited to no" ability to hold employees accountable successfully. On the other hand, 91 percent of respondents said they would rank "improving the ability to hold others accountable in an effective way" as one of the top leadership development needs of their organization (Starner 2015).[5] In addition to this, research suggests that 70 percent of employees (Brandon Hall Group2019)[6] feel their managers aren't objective in how they evaluate their performance. And it comes as no surprise that 69 percent of employees (Tiny Pulse 2017)[7] don't feel they're living up to their potential at work. This reinforces the need to think differently about managing performance at work.

The answer surely is to create an environment where employees are asked to reflect on their own performance more so. Having completed a body of work, done a task, or finished a project, the manager should ask the employee questions like:

- What went well in your opinion?
- What didn't go so well?
- What would you go differently next time?

By asking these sorts of questions, as Ron Carucci, author of *To Be Honest* says,

> reestablishes the connection between contribution and contributor. For decades, in an attempt at creating fairness, conventional thinking has kept the evaluation of work separate from the evaluation of people. This made sense when people were producing large volumes of the same output. But in a knowledge economy, people's ideas, creativity, and analysis are direct reflections of who they are—the nature of today's work makes accountability personal.[8]

Carucci's argument goes to the heart of why we need to shift from appraisal to performance development and use the vehicle of the conversation as the tool to do so.

Where the Rubber Meets the Road

Being Human

Author, Ron Carucci spoke with Hubert Joly, a former CEO of Best Buy, whose acclaimed turnaround of the retailer is well known. Key to that transformation was a new focus on helping individuals be themselves, to "be human." As Joly told Carucci:

> "When I first started as CEO, and they showed me the forms to fill out about my team's performance, and they wanted me to put numbers in boxes, I thought, why would anyone do this? I decided to simply ask people, 'How do you feel things went?'—and they would often be harder on themselves than I would have. I would ask, 'What do you need from me?'— and they would tell me. It seemed like a much more human approach to holding people accountable."[9]

There are many frameworks out there to support this shift. My own approach is the *Five Conversations Framework*. I'll finish this chapter by briefly explaining it to you. You will find more detail in my book, *Bring the Human Being Back to Work: The 10 Performance and Development Conversations Leaders Must Have.*[10] The *Five Conversations Framework* is one of many that will do the job.

The *Five Conversation Framework* was designed as a substitute to replace the performance review. It can also be used as an enabler to develop an ongoing development dialog. Many organizations are rightly reviewing their performance review, as I stated earlier.

Essentially, the *Five Conversations Framework* is based on five conversations, one per month, for five consecutive months. These conversations are developmental conversations. The following Figure is an illustration of the framework (Figure 16.1).

Let's look at each conversation briefly.

Timeframe	Conversation	Content
Month 1	Climate review conversation	• Job satisfaction, morale and communication
Month 2	Strengths ans talents conversation	• The effective use of strengths and talents now and in the future
Month 3	Opportunities for growth conversation	• Improveemnt of performance on-the-job
Month 4	Learning and development conversation	• Growth opportunities and support
Month 5	Innovation and continuous improvement conversation	• Improving workplace efficiencies and effectiveness

Figure 16.1 Five conversations framework

Climate Review Conversation

A climate review has nothing to do with the weather! It's designed to gauge the current atmosphere in the workplace. Specifically, it's concerned with employees' job satisfaction, the morale in the team, and the quality of communication. Although people's opinion about these matters can and often do fluctuate over the course of a year, it can be useful to take a snapshot of the business occasionally. By having a conversation with direct reports about the state of the current climate, managers have a handle on the current state of the business, and what needs to be done to improve the fundamentals of satisfaction, morale, and communication. Listening and responding to this feedback is a good place to start.

Strengths and Talents Conversation

Most appraisals focus on what's going wrong. They emphasis weaknesses and by-pass strengths and talents, in other words. Tom Rath in the # 1 *Wall Street Journal* bestseller: *Strengths Finder 2.0* underscores the value of a strengths and talent conversation:

> Society's relentless focus on people's shortcomings has turned into a global obsession. What's more, we have discovered that people have several times more potential for growth when they invest energy in developing their strengths instead of correcting their deficiencies. (Rath 2007)[11]

Apart from being an edifying place to start discussing a person's performance, this conversation capitalizes on people's innate talents. As the positive psychology movement has preached for two decades: Building upon strengths has a higher payoff then working on overcoming weaknesses (Ackerman 2020).[12]

Opportunities for Growth Conversation

This conversation invites an opportunity for employees to consider how they can improve their own work performance in KRAs. By doing so, the potential for the manager and team member to gain a common perspective on areas for improved performance is possible. A dual understanding of current and expected standards performance is an important first step.

The second step is to discuss and agree upon some tangible ways and means of improving the employee's performance to match expectations.

Thirdly and finally, this conversation is important in aligning performance expectations with the strategic direction of the business. Some opportunities identified can be put into practice straight away. And others can be adopted with more L&D support later.

Learning and Development Conversation

Conversations about L&D build on the previous two conversations. What learning experiences can assist in maximizing strengths and lifting performance in critical areas? Learning experiences, as we discussed in Chapter 10 can be job-, machine-, person-, or problem-centered. All four dimensions are important, as I've suggested.

Innovation and Continuous Improvement Conversation

This conversation is about discussing practical suggestions for improving the efficiency and effectiveness of the workplace. What can we do to improve our working environment? is the focus here.

Imagine for a moment the power of this conversation occurring across an organization during a particular month. Some of the ideas that surface will undoubtedly be too costly or impractical. But some would also be worth considering.

Each of these five conversations ought to take 20 minutes. Some go longer. Being thematically based, they are focused and therefore need not take a considerable amount of time.

Being more relaxed and conversational compared with the rigid appraisal regime, this new approach minimizes the power dynamic of the manager–employee relationship. The manager still asked questions to guide the conversation. But in this framework, the manager's role is converser and facilitator, not appraiser and assessor. This approach shifts the emphasis from appraising to developing people at work.

Several organizations I have worked with have replaced their old appraisal system with the *Five Conversations Framework*. In applying the framework, each manager in these enterprises is committing to 10 (two rounds of the five conversations) short but important conversations with each of his or her direct reports every year. This is likely to encourage more dialog between managers and staff than is currently occurring in most businesses. It also shifts the accountability for performance to the employee.

In the final chapter of PART 4, we look at the concept of human spirit and work and step away from our overreliance on extrinsic motivation.

Ten Key Takeaways

1. Performance appraisals typically come around once or twice a year and they are usually not something that everyone looks forward to.
2. What the boss thinks, irrespective of whether they are right or wrong, carries greater weight than the recipient.
3. Irrespective of the manager's interpersonal skills, these meetings are still controlled by the manager.
4. There are several inherent problems with this conventional appraisal system.
5. The performance review was designed to achieve two purposes. One purpose is to justify salary decisions. The second purpose is to increase performance.
6. A healthy working relationship—or any relationship—is based on a shared set of expectations.
7. Collaborative leaders understand the value of regular catch-ups with their team members.
8. How do we make employees more accountable for their performance? This is a perennial challenge that's not helped by an archaic performance management system.
9. The Five Conversation Framework was designed as a substitute to replace the performance review.
10. Being more relaxed and conversational compared with the rigid appraisal regime; this new approach minimizes the power dynamic of the manager–employee relationship.

CHAPTER 17

Shift 12: Carrot and Stick to Human Spirit and Work

Managers relying too much on extrinsic motivators to control behavior reinforces the employees' dependency on the leader to provide the rewards.

Stanford University researcher Mark Lepper and his team conducted a significant research study in the early 1970s, concerned with the impact of extrinsic rewards on performance. Specifically, Lepper was interested in whether prizes influence behavior in young children.

A brand-new activity was introduced to the children at a nursery. The teachers issued the children with creamy white artist's drawing paper and brand-new marker pens; the children were given time to draw with these novel materials. They had never done drawings with marker pens before.

Predictably, the children took to the activity with relish. But after exactly one hour, the materials were whisked away to the disappointment of the children.

Several days later, one of the researchers returned to the class and randomly divided the class into two groups to continue the new drawing activity. One group of children were taken to another room. They were given the opportunity to continue their drawings just as they had done before. After an hour, the researcher thanked the children in this group and took away the art material and their drawings. The second group of children were offered a prize for drawing their pictures.

It was explained to this group that some special prizes would be given to the children who drew good pictures. The children took to their task, anticipating they might receive a prize for their picture. This control group was given the same amount of time (one hour) as the other group to compete their artwork. At the end of the session, the researcher thanked the children as he'd done with the other group. But this time, he handed out a prize to each child in the control group.

One week later the researchers returned to the classroom. The afternoon period consisted of "free time;" the children could choose what they wanted to do with their time. The special paper and marker pens were placed on the tables and easily accessible for the children. However, the children had other options too. They could go outside and run around in the playground. They could play with the toys in the classroom. Or they could return to the drawing activity. The researchers observed the time the children spent on their chosen activities. To what extent would the prizes given to the children in the control group affect their choices and behavior? The researchers assumed that the children in the control group, who had received prizes, would spend more time on the drawing activity.

But that didn't happen!

The result was one the researchers didn't foresee. Their findings challenged conventional wisdom about parenting and education. The children who received the extrinsic rewards for their artwork chose to spend less time drawing than those who weren't rewarded. Conversely, the children who didn't receive a prize chose to spend more of their discretionary time on the drawing activity. The children who were rewarded seemed reluctant to continue with the activity without the promise of a further reward. The initial reward paradoxically reduced the children's motivation rather than increasing it.

But what was even more surprising is this: The artwork of all the children was evaluated by a group of independent judges with no knowledge of the experiment. The result was that the pictures drawn by the children who were rewarded were evaluated as less competent than the pictures drawn by the unrewarded group.

So, in summary: The children who received an extrinsic reward spent less time drawing when given a choice—and when they were rewarded, they put in less effort too. (Yeung 2011)[1]

This is the last chapter of PART 4: the rewarding phase of the employee lifecycle. In this chapter, I want to urge you to consider the rewards systems we use to motivate our people. There's too much emphasis placed on extrinsic and too little on intrinsic motivation. I've left this discussion at the end of the rewarding phase because all 13 mindset shifts (including the one in PART 5) have a common theme. All 13 mindset shifts, apart from being more employee-centered, stress the importance of intrinsic over extrinsic motivation. Therefore, I've left the concept of extrinsic rewards to last. I'll briefly summarize the connection between intrinsic motivation and the other mindset shifts we've covered at the end of this chapter, before addressing the final shift in PART 5.

Job Satisfaction and Extrinsic Rewards

Is it true that being satisfied with your work means you perform better? There's a widely held belief that satisfaction and performance go together. The pathway to better job performance—according to many managers—is through greater job satisfaction. This general belief has been around for at least 100 years, despite inconclusive evidence of a link between job satisfaction and job performance.

This misguided conviction has led to a range of performance management measures designed to satisfy people at work. So, we use extrinsic rewards—such as money, recognition, and praise—to foster a sense of satisfaction on the job.

What's needed to increase and sustain job performance, however, is cultivating the right workplace environment for intrinsic motivation to flourish. Engaged *hearts and minds* is an entirely different source of motivation from the satisfaction derived from the extrinsic rewards associated with a job. It's time we rethink rewards and its impact on performance.

Admittedly, one or two studies show a causal link between job satisfaction and job performance (Keaveney and Nelson 1993).[2] More studies show a reverse relationship; that is, performance leads to satisfaction on the job (Brown, Cron, and Leigh 1993; Darden, Hampton, and Howell 1989; and MacKenzie, Podsakoff, and Ahearne 1998).[3] But the clear majority of research concludes that too many other factors are in play to make the generalized claim that a satisfied employee is a higher performing employee (Judge, Bono, Thoresen, and Patton 2001).[4] And lots of studies show no relationship between satisfaction and performance (Judge, Bono, Thoresen, and Patton 2001).[5] So all the research taken together suggests we should look to other means to boost performance besides satisfying the employee with extrinsic rewards.

Extrinsic motivators come in two forms: rewards and punishments, commonly referred to the carrot and stick. These extrinsic rewards are typically money, recognition, and praise. Examples of punishments are criticism, withholding rewards, and a reprimand (Reilly 2017).[6] Extrinsic motivators come from someone other than the person they are targeted to motivate. It's a form of control, imposed on the workforce. The assumption supporting the carrot and stick approach is that by doing what the company or manager wants, you get rewarded. And if you don't meet this criterion, you don't get rewarded, and may get punished.

Several studies, including the one at the beginning of this chapter, suggest that extrinsic rewards aren't always effective, and can be counterproductive. Extrinsic motivators do, however, have their place. An overreliance on extrinsic motivators is characteristic of the traditional employment relationship we discussed in Chapter 9.

Managers relying too much on extrinsic motivators to control behavior reinforce the employees' dependency on the leader to provide the rewards. By focusing too much on outcomes that meet certain benchmarks, managers create a culture where employees understandably focus on the result to receive a reward (Reilly 2017).[7] In some cases, this is useful and effective. But the downside is that this fosters a dependency on the manager for rewards. It doesn't promote personal accountability and responsibility.

Where the Rubber Meets the Road

Rewarding the Dog for Chewing the Rug

Henry Kissinger tells a story about an incident that happened when he was advising President Nixon. Kissinger and Nixon were in the Oval Office discussing Middle East negotiations but could make no progress because Nixon's dog was chewing and barking at the rug. In frustration, Nixon reached into his desk and threw a bone to the dog. Upon seeing this, Kissinger said to Mr. Nixon, "Mr. President, you have just taught your dog to chew rugs." (Reilly 2017)[8]

Intrinsic Motivation

Intrinsic behaviors are driven and defined by the employee, as distinct from extrinsic rewards. Put simply, intrinsic motivation is self-motivation. Performance is driven by the person, not someone else. Furthermore, the intrinsically motivated person feels a deeper sense of personal accomplishment. Achievement can be dampened when the employee does it for the external reward. What's more, the carrot and stick narrow the employee's focus to self-interest, which isn't conducive to fostering collaboration and teamwork.

The answer to getting the best from people at work is literally under our nose, as I said in Chapter 3. It's the work itself that has the greatest potential to improve personal productivity. Instead of driving performance with extrinsic methods, generating intrinsic motivation through the type of work done and how it's done has enormous, largely untapped potential.

In PART 3, we talked about several measures for making work more appealing. Greater a focus on nonjob roles, job crafting, and opening opportunities for collaborative intelligence through super teams, are ways to make the work people do attractive and more productive. These strategies liberate intrinsic motivation.

Getting back to the discussion about job satisfaction, there's no doubting that a satisfied employee is better off than a dissatisfied employee. Nevertheless, I need to challenge this deeply rooted belief that extrinsic rewards bring the best out of people. Sometimes the carrot and stick does get good results—they can be effective, now, and again. But extrinsic rewards aren't the only way. For sustained performance, the questions we need to ask are:

- How can we engage the heart and mind of the employee in their work?
- How can we connect human spirit and work?

One of the main criticisms from *humanists*,[9] about the application of scientific management principles is its dehumanization of people at work. By separating the planning function from the execution of the work, the employee needn't bother to think—the thinking part has already been done by management. This division of planning and doing—as logical as it appears—strips the employee of their autonomy and deprives them of their self-sufficiency.

Mastery of work in these circumstances, even in work that is classified as *skilled* or *professional*, is reduced to repetitiously following a series of processes or procedures. Work that's broken down into small, controllable segments, is often considered meaningless by the jobholder. I think the humanist movement has a valid point.

It's not only the process of work, but its meaning that can be problematic. Dave and Wendy Ulrich, in their book *The Why of Work: How Great Leaders Build Abundant Organizations That Win*, explain the significance of understanding how work contributes to a greater cause beyond simply completing a process.[10] Although I acknowledged that the nature of work is profoundly different from the days of the factory assembly line, performance management practices we use haven't kept pace. Work is still organized into specifications and tightly controlled and monitored by a regime of KPIs and targets. A variety of carrots and sticks are used to "motivate" the jobholder.

Dan Pink in his popular book, *Drive: The Surprising Truth About What Motivates Us*, challenges us to think completely differently about human motivation and performance (Pink 2009).[11] Pink tells us that the carrot and stick approach isn't always effective, especially for the relatively new breed of knowledge worker. He claims we need to do more than satisfy the employee with a sprinkling of external rewards. And I think he's right—as a growing number of authors do.

High performance, Pink argues, doesn't stem from the promise of rewards and incentives for following a set of predetermined systems and processes. As he puts it:

> For as long as any of us can remember, we've configured our organizations and constructed our lives around its bedrock assumption: The way to improve performance, increase productivity, and encourage excellence is to reward the good and punish the bad. (Pink 2009)[12]

People generally want and need more from their work than just a job. But instead, people are now aware there's "no long-term." The widening gulf between turmoil in the marketplace and the growing need for what famous psychologist Abraham Maslow describes as *self-actualization*, is causing great stress in workplaces everywhere.

On the one hand, the trends in Western society for the humanization of the workplace heighten the hunger for meaningful working environments. But on the other hand, marketplace volatility makes it ever more challenging for employees and employers to respectively seek and provide meaningful work. Perhaps this extending chasm may partially explain the continual practice of using extrinsic motivational tools to keep the employee satisfied.

Extrinsic rewards are less effective than previously thought. And there's no doubting that people want more from their work than the promise of bonuses. There are opportunities for HR to shift the emphasis from extrinsic to intrinsic reward structures through the design of work.

Work promises so much more than a source of income—it's potentially a vehicle for fostering personal growth, well-being, and purpose. When external rewards are used, like bonuses, to fuel better performance, it paradoxically takes the jobholder's attention off the work the reward is designed to improve. The promise of a bonus shifts the jobholder's focus from the task to the prize. Put simply, the work is a means to an end—a reward.

Refer to the research at the beginning of this chapter. Extrinsic rewards can reduce, not increase performance. With the bonus top-of-mind, it's unsurprisingly common for employees to cut corners, do whatever it takes, or even cheat to get their hands on the prize. As well intended as they are—and as effective as they can sometimes be—extrinsic rewards can back-fire and be counterproductive too.

The idea of using reward and punishment to induce greater performance is deeply rooted in our psyche, as I've mentioned. Workers were once viewed as a cog in the factory machine. Bonus pay was issued to workers who performed the right work, the right way, within the right timeframe. Worker conformity was part of the machinery of the factory. The carrot and the stick were the levers to reinforce orthodoxy. Today, we perpetuate this approach; we try to motivate employees with a suite of rewards and the occasional sanction. Little has changed in the way we kindle performance, even though the work we do is entirely different.

The underlying belief is that the best (some would say, the only) way to enforce performance is to reward and punish work behaviors (or lack of behaviors). But if a job's only real purpose is to receive a wage and the occasional bonus, then this won't be enough. Without any real sense of freedom and self-sufficiency, or opportunities to grow and develop, work can't promote the employee's well-being past paying the bills. Though an employee may feel satisfied with this arrangement, it's hardly likely to lead to inspired work performance. A new game plan is needed.

Satisfying employees with extrinsic rewards is necessary. But it's not the only way. Sustained performance, without relying on external stimuli, can originate from the personal satisfaction one gets from the work they do. There's a widely held management myth, however, that the carrot and stick is the only way to fuel work performance. Striving to capture the human spirit in work is ignored on the assumption that it's futile. Yet it's a powerful and viable motivator in most things in people's lives.

Daniel Pink suggests three ways of fostering natural motivation at work:

- Give people more freedom and the autonomy to make their own decisions about the work they do.
- Provide people with opportunities to grow and develop.
- Explain the purpose of the work people do.

As Pink reminds us, "we have a deep-seated desire to direct our own lives, to extend and expand our abilities, and live a life of purpose" (Pink 2009).[13]

I want to now make a connection between intrinsic motivation and the mindset shifts we've covered so far in the book. So far, we have looked at mindset shifts in the starting, developing, and rewarding phases of the employee lifecycle. We have one more phase to consider: the parting phase in PART 5.

Beginning with the starting phase (Shift 1: Past performance to future potential), I make the point that the attributes of potential should be considered in the selection decision. The attributes we identified in Chapter 6 are all based on personal motivation. In Shift 2 (Induction to integration), the premise supporting integration is to provide the new hire with more responsibility for their onboarding experience. For Shift 3 (Onsite to hybrid working), in preparation for hybrid working arrangements, working remotely, by its nature, requires a greater degree of self-motivation. In Shift 4 (Them and us to collaboration), transitioning from the traditional to new employment relationship, emphasizes the need for the employee to take more responsibility in a partnership arrangement.

In the developing phase of employment, Shift 5 (Training to multidimensional learning), is designed to develop a broader array of capabilities beyond preparing one to better execute their technical job skills. For Shifts 6 and 7, the focus was on the importance of developing nonjob attributes. The four nonjob roles I suggest are self-initiated and require intrinsic motivation. Shift 8 (Job design to job redesign) illustrated how job crafting can enhance the design of work. Since job crafting is employee initiated, it encourages personal initiative and motivation. In Shift 9 (Competition to collaboration), I discussed the idea of moving from competing to collaborating with machines in super teams. The super team structure promotes self-direction.

Then we moved to the rewarding phase of employment. Shift 10 (Technical knowhow to people leadership) emphasizes promoting people to leadership roles on their interpersonal skills and personal attributes. And finally in Shift 11 (Appraising to developing performance), we discussed the importance of personal accountability in performance. So, you can see that intrinsic motivation is fundamental to all these mindset shifts.

This is the end of PART 4. In PART 5, we look at one more shift required in the employee lifestyle: building networks and staying connected to past employees.

Ten Key Takeaways

1. There's a widely held belief that satisfaction and performance go together.
2. Extrinsic motivators come in two forms: rewards and punishments, commonly referred to the carrot and stick.

3. Several studies suggest that extrinsic rewards aren't always effective and can be counterproductive.

4. Intrinsic behaviors are driven and defined by the employee, as distinct from extrinsic rewards.

5. It's the work itself that has the greatest potential to improve personal productivity.

6. Greater focus on nonjob roles, job crafting, and opening opportunities for collaborative intelligence through super teams, are ways to make the work people attractive and more productive.

7. Mastery of work, even in work that is classified as skilled or professional, is reduced to repetitiously following a series of processes or procedures.

8. It's not only the process of work, but its meaning that can be problematic.

9. People generally want and need more from their work than just a job.

10. Work promises so much more than a source of income—it's potentially a vehicle for fostering personal growth, well-being, and purpose.

PART 5

Parting Phase of Employment

CHAPTER 18

Shift 13: Exit Interviews to Building Networks

Business is now recognizing—while lifetime employment is a thing of the past—that there's value in maintaining a lifelong relationship with former employees.

> Your phone rings. It's a number you don't recognize. You agonize for a moment about whether to pick up, and when you do, your fears are at once confirmed: It's a student from your alma mater reaching out to request a donation. Yep, you've learned your lesson: No more answering calls from unknown numbers.
>
> But let's take a minute to reimagine that situation. What if it wasn't your university that was trying to get in touch, but, instead, a former employer? And what if they weren't asking for money, but were inviting you to an exclusive networking event or, even better, proposing an enticing new job opportunity? You'd be a lot more likely to pick up, right?
>
> This isn't some far-fetched scenario—it's already happening. Many companies are recognizing the advantages of keeping relationships with their former employees and are doing so. Companies can not only gain valuable insight into the company's triumphs and failures as an organization but can also turn former employees into engaged brand ambassadors for life. Sound enticing? See potential value for your company?[1]

The final phase of the employee lifecycle is the parting phase. Or is it? The *parting* phase can be misleading. This phase may be temporary as more and more employers are inviting high-performing employees back on short-term projects, or for reemployed. In this final chapter, we consider the shift from the exit interview to building and accessing an alumni network. In the past, the exit interview preceded by a farewell morning tea was the end of a chapter in an employee's life.

In Chapter 9, one of the changing expectations from the traditional to new psychological contract is a transition from *loyalty* to *commitment*. For most of the 20th century the employment compact was based on loyalty. Loyalty was the employer promise of lifetime employment in exchange for the employee complying with the ethos of the company. This expectation as we know isn't valid anymore.

Lifelong employment and loyalty are no longer realistic in today's world. Making the promise of a permanent job is not only unrealistic but it also breaches trust with a new hire. For an employer to promise this now is a lie.

Commitment is a more practical expectation than loyalty. As a shared expectation between manager and employee, commitment has a different orientation. Commitment in this context is *you scratch my back and I'll scratch yours*. In practice, this new expectation involves the employee adding value to the organization. And in return, the employer offers the employee the opportunity to grow and develop and become more employable.

This changing expectation is fueled by the realization that jobs are no longer permanent. Although commitment extends further. A workable new compact encourages a lasting alliance between employee and employer past a job. Both entities in the employment relationship can add value to each other in other ways. "Employees invest in the company's adaptability; the company invests in employees' employability" (Hoffman, Casnocha, and Yeh 2013).[2] Reid Hoffman, cofounder of LinkedIn, conceptualizes this new relationship as a "tour of duty."[3]

The tour of duty approach, on the one hand, involves the company getting an engaged employee who produces tangible results for the firm for a period. On the other hand, the employee is viewed as an important advocate and potential resource at the end of their tour of duty, namely, when they move on from their current job. The tour of duty concept, if properly implemented, provides a clear foundation for both partners to work together, even after the employee leaves to work elsewhere.

Building Alumni Networks

Deloitte's refer to their alumni as "colleagues for life." Other companies use terms such as "boomerang employees" or "comeback colleagues." There's growing support for companies to build alumni networks. Business is now recognizing—while lifetime employment is outdated—that there's value in maintaining a lifelong relationship with former employees. A 2018 LinkedIn study showed that in the earlier decade, the U.S. national rate of workplace *boomerangs* had more than doubled, hitting nearly 3 percent by the first half of 2018. In some organizations, it's well into double figures.[4]

As this trend continues, it incentivizes companies to create and build connections with past employees. These networks can rapidly and easily reemployed past employees who have showed a proven record.

The stigma associated with ex-employees is changing. More employers are paying attention to these past employees, particularly as possible rehires. A 2015 survey conducted by the Workforce Institute at Kronos Inc. and WorkplaceTrends.com found that 76 percent of more than 1,800 HR professionals reported being more open to hiring former employees than they were in the past (Businesswire 2015).[5]

Former employees—if they leave on good terms—can be a rich source of brand ambassadors, potential clients, future business partners, and top-notch rehires. Like university administrators enthusiastically welcome former students back to their campus community, companies are following suit. HR leaders and managers are reaching out to individuals who left their jobs, excluding, of course, poor performers. Companies are finding lasting benefits staying connected to past employees (Tucker 2018).[6]

Although alumni networks are not new to the corporate world, there has been a renewed interest in growing them in recent years. The professional services industry—which includes legal, consulting, and accounting firms—has long led the way in creating and nurturing networks of former employees.

Conenza is a Seattle-based company that helps businesses build and manage their alumni networks. Their recent report found that 22 percent of the more than 60 survey respondents have successful alumni programs for at least 10 years. Large financial services companies such as Citigroup and JPMorgan are among the early adopters, followed by technology companies such as SAP and Dell. Nonprofits and mission-driven organizations, including the Bill & Melinda Gates Foundation and Junior Achievement Worldwide, also now rely heavily on alumni networks (Tucker 2018).[7] As Conenza's CEO and founder Tony Audino, who worked at Microsoft 20 years ago and helped that company develop its alumni network says, "more than 20 percent of workers change roles every year. That kind of disruption in the workforce is only going to increase" (Tucker 2018).[8]

One of the primary drivers behind the growth of these alumni programs is the recognition that people switch jobs much more frequently than they did in the past. Apart from 20 percent of employee turnover a year, there are approximately 10,000 Baby Boomers who retire every day. Millennials move to different positions every 2.8 years, on average (Tucker 2018).[9] This clearly isn't a passing phase.

These movements in the job market drain companies of corporate knowledge. As senior employees exit, they leave behind a knowledge deficit. According to Chris Hoyt, president of CareerXroads, a talent acquisition consultancy in Hurst, Texas, "a lot of these alumni programs are an effort to close that gap through rehiring, professional development and coaching opportunities" (Tucker 2018).[10] This is another driver for the rise in alumni networks.

Companies that invest in lifelong relationships with their employees have a competitive edge. The alumni network is their tool to support a connection with past employees. It's therefore unsurprising that 98 percent of the Fortune 500 is having some form of an alumni program.[11] Although smaller companies are slow to embrace this mindset shift.

The collaborative employment relationship I described in Chapter 9 isn't confined to the job the employee is hired to do. It's developing into a lifelong partnership between the individual and organization based on mutual benefit.

If a firm encourages employees to be entrepreneurial, won't they be encouraged to leave? The answer is yes, some will. But the point is this: Retaining those entrepreneurial employees, even for a limited time, can reap enormous benefits for the company. We should accept that regardless

Where the Rubber Meets the Road

Do Entrepreneurial Employees Really Benefit Their Employers?

Entrepreneurial employees can be extremely valuable, as John Lasseter's story demonstrates.

In the early 1980s, Lasseter, then a young animator at Disney, pitched his superiors on the new technology of computer-generated animation—and was promptly fired. He ended up in Lucasfilm's computer graphics division, which Steve Jobs acquired and, with Lasseter's help, built into the computer-generated-animation powerhouse Pixar. In 2006, Disney paid $7.4 billion for Pixar and named Lasseter chief creative officer of both Pixar and Walt Disney Animation Studios. Disney learned an expensive lesson: It would have been much cheaper to let Lasseter exercise his creative and entrepreneurial genius in-house. (Hoffman, Casnocha, and Yeh 2013)[12]

of how many smart employees a company has, there are always more smart people working outside the company then within.

This brings us to the central point about building alumni networks. By actively building alumni of past employees, the company can still engage entrepreneurial employees outside the company through their alumni network. Talented employees know other talented employees, even if they're hired in other companies. An alumnus creates leverage.

Entrepreneurs who have a diverse network of friends and colleagues compared with those that don't are likely to be three times more innovative. Martin Ruef, who analyzed the social and business relations of 766 graduates of the Stanford Business School, found that those entrepreneurs with the most diverse friendships scored three times higher on metric of innovation. This suggests that pooling together diverse ideas can cultivate innovation (Schawbel 2012).[13]

It therefore makes sense for companies to encourage their current employees to build and maintain professional networks outside the organization. Instead of assuming it's an act of untrustworthiness, an employee who keeps their LinkedIn profile up to date or has a massive following on Twitter is potentially an asset for their current employer. Encouraging current employees to build their business networks should be viewed as a positive development.

HubSpot, a Massachusetts-based marketing software company, for example, uses an internal company Wiki to stimulate networking. If you mentioned on the website that you're interested in a book, it's very possible that the book could end up in your Kindle shortly after from a colleague. Furthermore, HubSpot urges their employees to take important people out to lunch at the company's expense. Bain's global director of career development and alumni relations, Cindy Lewiton Jackson, sums up this mentality: "The goal is not to retain employees. The goal is to build lifelong affiliation." (Hoffman, Casnocha, and Yeh 2013)[14]

Establishing an alumni network isn't a sign that you can't retain talent. It's just facing reality. People are spending less and less time with the one employer. What's more, a past employee is likely to be networking informally with other employees anyway. By developing an alumni network, the company is having a voice in the process. So, it makes good business sense.

Losing a talented employee to a competitor was painful for the company. It may feel like a rejection and the departing employee can suffer the cold shoulder. But as Forbes contributor, Maynard Webb says:

> The fact is, we don't own our people; they choose to work for us, and we choose to hire them. It is our obligation to do everything we can to make them better while they are with us. It is the employee's obligation to do everything they can to make the company successful. (Webb 2017)[15]

This is a more pragmatic approach to adopt.

In summary, alumni programs allow a company to sustain a mutually beneficial relationship with their former employees. These past employees can be called upon for short- or longer-term re-employment in the future. A well-run alumni program gives the business the opportunity to stay in contact and a possible mechanism for recruiting them back effortlessly, and at no cost quickly, if needed.

The primary reason to develop an alumni program is recruitment related. But a well-designed corporate alumni network can benefit a company in other ways. Investing in corporate alumni programs can also build sales leads and open doors for business growth.

From an HR perspective, the alumni network has several benefits. First, it improves the quality of candidates by rehiring top performers. This reduces the costs of recruitment and selection and the impact of job lag (I discussed the costs of job lag in Chapter 7). Second, it increases the number and quality of employee referrals by expanding the program to include alumni. Third, it strengthens the employer brand image through the industry. Fourth, it can boost retention among current employees, by developing a stronger positive image. And fifth, it creates a pool of talent available to mentor current employees.[16] A well-designed corporate alumni network can benefit the organization in so many ways.

Maynard Webb outlines some steps that can be taken to build an alumni network that works. When people leave, thank them for their service and acknowledge their contribution. Assist them to stay in contact. Create an alumni page on Facebook and LinkedIn. Update alumni regularly on the company and what it's doing. Exchange job opportunities. Host the occasional alumni event and invite former employees to attend (Webb 2017).[17] These are simple steps that benefit everyone.

This is the end of the parting phase of employment. I hope you found the 13 mindset shifts thought-provoking and useful. Following is an action plan that you might find helpful to implement some of the changes I advocate in the book.

Ten Key Takeaways

1. Lifelong employment and loyalty are no longer realistic in today's world.
2. There's growing support for companies to build alumni networks.
3. The stigma associated with ex-employees is changing.
4. Former employees—if they leave on good terms—can be a rich source of brand ambassadors, potential clients, future business partners, and top-notch rehires.
5. One of the primary drivers behind the growth of these alumni programs is the recognition that people switch jobs much more frequently than they did in the past.

6. These movements in the job market drain companies of corporate knowledge.

7. Companies that invest in lifelong relationships with their employees have a competitive edge.

8. By actively building alumni of past employees, the company can still engage entrepreneurial employees outside the company through their alumni network.

9. Establishing an alumni network isn't a sign that you can't retain talent. It's just facing reality.

10. The primary reason to develop an alumni program is recruitment related. But a well-designed corporate alumni network can benefit a company in other ways.

Action Plan

In this action plan, I want to make it easier for you to implement the 13 mindset shifts I have discussed throughout the book. Following is a checklist to evaluate your own organization. You can work your way through methodically from the first phase of the employee lifecycle to the last phase. From your appraisal, you can then apply the necessary changes.

You can do this more thoroughly by applying an organizationwide-survey tool. By using a 360-degree evaluation, you are likely to get a more accurate and thorough review across the business, by inviting everyone to participate. If you'd like more information about this methodology, you are welcome to contact me, and we can assist you to administer the 360-degree feedback evaluation and subsequent report.[1]

As a reminder, here is the employee lifecycle framework in Figure A.1 that I shared with you in Chapter 4.

For the action plan, the focus is on the eight HR practices covered in the employee lifecycle framework. The following Table A.1 illustrates the 13 mindset shifts and their corresponding phases in the employee lifecycle.

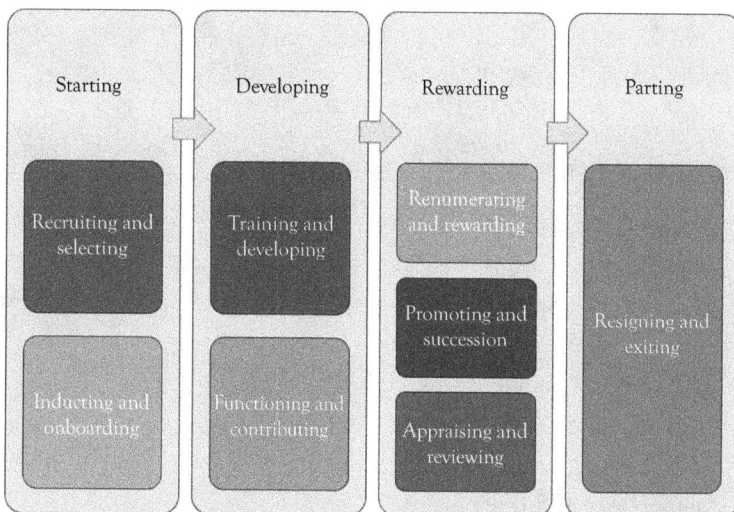

Starting	Developing	Rewarding	Parting
Recruiting and selecting	Training and developing	Renumerating and rewarding	Resigning and exiting
		Promoting and succession	
Inducting and onboarding	Functioning and contributing	Appraising and reviewing	

Figure A.1 Employee lifecycle framework

Table A.1 HR mindset shifts

Phases	Mindset shifts	
	Current	Future
Starting	Shift 1—past behavior	future potential
	Shift 2—onboarding	integration
	Shift 3—onsite	hybrid working
	Shift 4—them and us	collaboration
Developing	Shift 5—training	multidimensional learning
	Shift 6—job	nonjob roles
	Shift 7—job description	role description
	Shift 8—job design	job redesign
	Shift 9—competition	partnership
Rewarding	Shift 10—technical knowhow	people leadership
	Shift 11—appraising	developing performance
	Shift 12—carrot and stick	human spirit and work
Parting	Shift 13—exit interviews	building networks

We'll take each of the 13 shifts and summarize the key points in the form of a series of five questions, for each shift. These five questions for each mindset shift are designed to focus your attention on whether elements of the new mentality have been fully embraced in your future. As I said earlier, it's likely that in some cases, your firm may be in transition between the *current* and *new* mindsets. So, for those questions where you can't confidently claim a *yes*, then that can be an area to spend more energy and resources.

Starting Phase of Employment

Shift 1: Past Performance to Future Potential

1. Have the attributes of future potential been defined in your recruitment and selection process?
2. Has the company sourced a diagnostic tool to assess candidates' future potential?
3. Have a set of questions been crafted to be used in interviews to assess future potential?
4. Has training been provided in the organization on the value and importance of future potential?

5. Is there a process to ask referees a series of questions on future potential?

Shift 2: Onboarding to Integration

6. Does the organization measure employee turnover in the first 90 days of employment?
7. Has HR developed a comprehensive integration phase to supplement the induction and onboarding process?
8. Is there an established program of regular check-ins between the manager and the new hire?
9. Is there a comprehensive training program for all employees and managers to train them on what to do in the integration phase?
10. Have managers been trained on the content and questions used in the integration phase of onboarding?

Shift 3: Onsite to a Hybrid Work Arrangement

11. Has the organization updated all its policies and procedures to accommodate hybrid working arrangements?
12. Are all L&D opportunities accessible remotely?
13. Have the communication systems been reviewed and tailored for remote working arrangements?
14. Have managers been trained to effectively lead remotely?
15. Does the organization have an effective induction, onboarding, and integration program for remote workers?

Shift 4: Them and Us to Collaboration

16. Does the organization mostly have managers who follow the eight expectations of the new employment relationship?
17. Is the organization's policies and procedures compatible with the new employment relationship expectations?
18. Are all managers being trained to cultivate a new mindset about leadership that reflects the collaborative employment relationship?

19. Are there indicators in place to assess how closely aligned the organization is to the eight new expectations of the collaborative employment relationship?

20. Is there a strategy in place to shift the organizational culture to reflect the eight new employment relationship expectations?

Developing Phase of Employment

Shift 5: Training to Multidimensional Learning

21. Has the L&D budget been reviewed to reflect an even distribution of expenditure for the four dimensions of learning?

22. Are relevant and effective programs for person-centered, problem-centered, and machine-centered learning available and accessible?

23. Are effective evaluation systems in place for each of the four dimensions of learning?

24. Are managers accessing programs across the four dimensions of learning?

25. Are employees sufficiently aware of the four dimensions of learning and their relevance for their career?

Shift 6: Job to Nonjob Roles

26. Has the importance and value of nonjob roles been adequately explained to the workforce?

27. Have nonjob roles being integrated into the work document?

28. Have all employees been consulted about the nonjob roles and how they apply to their work?

29. Have KPIs being established for each of the nonjob roles?

30. Are managers giving regular feedback on the nonjob roles?

Shift 7: Job Description to Role Description

31. Is there evidence that managers are discussing the role of positive attitude and enthusiasm with their team members?

32. Are managers discussing the relevance and importance of the team role with their team members?

33. Is there sufficient evidence that employees are taking opportunities to upgrading their skills and capabilities?

34. Are there more suggestions and ideas of ways of making the organization more efficient and effective coming from employees?

35. Is there generally more discussion about nonjob roles throughout the organization?

Shift 8: Job Design to Redesign

36. Has a job crafting program across the organization been implemented?

37. Are managers encouraging the benefits of job crafting?

38. Are all three dimensions of job crafting (task, relational, and cognitive) evident?

39. Are there good illustrations of job crafting that can be used as examples for other teams?

40. Is there tangible evidence of job crafting throughout the organization?

Shift 9: Competing to Partnership

41. Is AI viewed as a partner or competitor for employment?

42. Is there evidence of more project-based teams then previously?

43. Has the organizational chart been rewritten to reflect the existence of project teams?

44. Have L&D opportunities increased for machine-centered learning?

45. Is your organization embracing super teams?

Rewarding Phase of Employment

Shift 10: Technical Knowhow to People Leadership

46. Is the succession planning program invested in people leadership development for future roles?

47. Is there evidence that internal leadership promotions are sufficiently focused on people skills?

48. Is the talent development program linked to the succession planning program?

49. Does the talent development program include identifying employees with potential?
50. Are managers consciously identifying and encouraging leadership potential talent in their teams?

Shift 11: Appraising to Developing Performance

51. Are training and development opportunities available for all managers on developmental conversations?
52. Has the organization implemented an ongoing developmental conversation framework?
53. Is there widespread evidence that people are using the framework and having regular check-ins with their team members?
54. Is there an ongoing evaluation of the effectiveness of the development conversation framework?
55. Is there widespread support for abolishing the annual performance review?

Shift 12: Carrot and Stick to Human Spirit and Work

56. Is your organization actively redressing the imbalance between extrinsic and intrinsic motivational reward?
57. Is there evidence that employees are taking more accountability for performance in the starting phase of their employment?
58. Is there evidence that the employment relationship is moving from a traditional to collaborative partnership?
59. Do employees exercise more autonomy in the work they do than previously?
60. Are internal leadership promotions based more on interpersonal skills than technical knowhow?

Parting Phase of Employment

Shift 13: Exit Interviews to Building Networks

61. Has your organization implemented an alumni network?
62. Is there evidence of a shift in attitude about departing employees to building networks??

63. Are employees encouraged to network?

64. Is the alumni network benefiting the individual and the organization?

65. Have former employees being rehired for work opportunities?

You can use these 65 questions to guide your observations throughout the organization. Or, if you want to get a more rigorous and thorough assessment, you can contact me to run this as a 360- degree feedback process.[2] This methodology can be used to compare the views of top management, middle management, and workforce and between the various functions in your organization. This report can give you a more comprehensive assessment of how effective these 13 mindset shifts are taking hold (or still stuck in the past). This will give you an opportunity to develop a more targeted plan-of-action for change.

This brings us to the end. I hope you found some useful tools and insights to improve your HR practices. *The Future of Human Resources* has given you a framework based on the employee lifecycle to make the necessary adjustments needed for the future. I would suggest that you start with one of the four phases first and then move on to the next phase. I wish you all the very best in your journey.

Thank you!

Thank you for joining me on the journey towards improving employee empowerment. I hope you have found
The Future of Human Resources: Unlocking Human Potential provoking and useful!
If you love the book and have a moment to spare, I would really appreciate a brief review on the site where you purchased the book.
Your help in spreading the word is gratefully received!

Need more help?
Organizational profile

If you wish to apply the organizational profile explained in the last chapter, please contact me direct at tim@winnersatwork.com.au and we can arrange this for you. It's reasonably priced too and it's a great place to start shifting the necessary mindsets.

Industry updates

If you would like to receive my monthly newsletter with interesting article and tools for leaders, please go to https://www.winnersatwork.com.au/latest-industry-updates/

Speaking and consulting

I speak regularly on this topic and others around the world. If you would like to engage me in your upcoming conference, contact me at tim@winnersatwork.com.au

I am also available for consulting work too.

Useful leadership tools

Go to www.winnersatwork.com.au for some useful tools to help you, your team, and organization.

Other books by Tim Baker

The 8 Values of Highly Productive Companies: Creating Wealth from a New Employment Relationship

The End of the Performance Review: A New Approach to Appraising Employee Performance

Attracting and Retaining Talent: Becoming an Employer of Choice

The New Influencing Toolbox: Capabilities for Communicating with Influence

Conversations at Work: Promoting a Culture of Conversation in a Changing Workplace

The End of the Job Description: Changing from a Job-focus to Performance-focus

Performance Management for Agile Organizations: Overthrowing the Eight Management Myths that Hold Businesses Back

Bringing the Human Being Back to Work: The 10 Performance and Development Conversations Leaders Must Have

Winning Teams: The Eight Characteristics of High Performing Teams

Breaking the Proactive Paradox: Maximizing Performance Through Empowerment

Mastering Feedback: A Practical Guide for Better Leadership Conversations

Mastering Influence: A Practical Guide for Better Leadership Conversations

Mastering Performance: A Practical Guide for Better Leadership Conversations

Mastering Change: A Practical Guide for Better Leadership Conversations

Mastering Meetings: A Practical Guide for Better Leadership Conversations

Mastering Conflict: A Practical Guide for Better Leadership Conversations

Notes

Introduction

1. Taylor (2006).
2. www.britannica.com/technology/Model-T

Chapter 1

1. Deloitte Insights (2021).
2. CEO Magazine (2019).
3. Deloitte Insights (2021).
4. Rokeach (1973).
5. Sneader and Sternfels (2020).
6. Sneader and Sternfels (2020).

Chapter 2

1. How Too. Top 3 HR trends in 2021.
2. Susskind (2020).
3. Susskind (2020).
4. Stapleton (2021).
5. Autor (2015).
6. Joseph, Lim, and Chun (2018).
7. Deutsch (2021).
8. Deutsch (2021).

Chapter 3

1. Deloitte Insights (2021).
2. Deloitte Insights (2021).
3. Baker (2018).
4. Morgan (2017).

Chapter 4

1. Johnson (2019).
2. Weber (2016).
3. Bradley and McDonald (2011).
4. Graeber (2018).
5. Miller (2021).

Chapter 5

1. Mercer (2019).
2. Murphy (2021).
3. Baker (2013).
4. Pink (2010).

Chapter 6

1. Ready, Conger, and June (2010).
2. Ready, Conger, and June (2010).
3. Ready, Conger, and June (2010).
4. www.thomas.co/assessments/workplace-personality-tests
5. Fernández-Aráoz (2014).
6. Fernández-Aráoz (2014).
7. On re-inventing HR page 122.

Chapter 7

1. Cable, Gino, and Staats (2013).
2. Baker (2014).
3. Baker (2014).
4. Work Institute (2019)
5. Cable, Gino, and Staats (2013).
6. www.akyra.com.au/induction-onboarding
7. Human Capital Institute (2019).
8. Investors in People, Available from www.investorsinpeople.com/ knowledge/onboarding-induction/
9. www.bqint.com/index.php/onboarding-isnt-enough/
10. Lombardi (2011).

Chapter 8

1. Root (2021).
2. Hubstaff blog (2020).
3. Hubstaff blog (2020).
4. Gallacher (2020).
5. www.forbes.com/sites/tracybrower/2021/01/17/think-productivity-with-work-from-home-is-improving-think-again-heres-what-you-must-know/?sh=51bb8aaa2d67
6. www.forbes.com/sites/tracybrower/2021/01/17/think-productivity-with-work-from-home-is-improving-think-again-heres-what-you-must-know/?sh=51bb8aaa2d67
7. Künn, Seel, and Zegners (2020).
8. Global Workplace Analytics (2019).
9. Acton (2017).
10. www.amazon.com/World-Without-Email-Reimagining-Communication-ebook/dp/B08BKSJX1M
11. Schneider (2018).
12. www.talentlms.com/blog/remote-work-statistics-survey/

Chapter 9

1. Baker (2014).
2. Baker (2014).
3. Middlemiss (2015).

Chapter 10

1. Baker (2014).
2. "Why Power Skills Are What You Need to Succeed." UBIS, Available from https://ubis-geneva.ch/blog/why-power-skills-are-what-you-need-to-succeed/
3. Baker (2009).

Chapter 11

1. N.A. (2006).
2. Baker (2016).

3. Peakson (2021).
4. Warner (2012).
5. Warner (2012).

Chapter 12

1. Baker (2016).
2. O'Hara (2017).
3. Baker (2016).

Chapter 13

1. Baker (2021).
2. Petrou, Demerouti, Peeters, Schaufeli, and Hetland (2012).
3. Berg, Dutton, and Wrzesniewski (2007).
4. Wrzesniewski, Berg, and Dutton (2010).
5. Caldwell and O'Reilly (1990).
6. Halbesleben (2010); Dubbelt, Demerouti, and Rispens (2019).
7. Dutton and Wrzesniewski (2020).
8. Baker (2021).

Chapter 14

1. Deloitte Global Human Capital Trends (2020).
2. N.A. (2019).
3. N.A. (2019).
4. N.A. (2019).
5. N.A. (2019).
6. Fountaine, McCarthy, and Saleh (2019).
7. Deloitte Global Human Capital Trends (2020).
8. Deloitte Global Human Capital Trends (2020).
9. Deloitte Global Human Capital Trends (2020).
10. Volini, et al. (2019).
11. N.A. (2019).
12. Deloitte Global Human Capital Trends (2020).
13. N.A. (2019).

Chapter 15

1. Welsh (2019).
2. Baker (2021).
3. Valcour (2021).
4. CIPD (2020).
5. Fernandez, Nagel, and Green (2021).
6. Fernandez, Nagel, and Green (2021).
7. Fernandez, Nagel, and Green (2021).
8. Candy (2021).

Chapter 16

1. Senge (2006).
2. Baker (2013).
3. Baker (2013).
4. Kouzes and Posner (2011).
5. Starner (2015).
6. Brandon Hall Group (2019).
7. Tiny Pulse (2017).
8. Carucci (2021).
9. Carucci (2020).
10. Baker (2018).
11. Rath (2007).
12. Ackerman (2020).

Chapter 17

1. Yeung (2011).
2. Keaveney and Nelson (1993); Shore and Martin (1989).
3. Brown, Cron, and Leigh (1993); Darden, Hampton, and Howell (1989); MacKenzie, Podsakoff, and Ahearne (1998).
4. Judge, Bono, Thoresen, and Patton (2001).
5. Judge, Bono, Thoresen, and Patton (2001).
6. Reilly (2017).
7. Reilly (2017).

8. Reilly (2017).
9. Humanism is a philosophical and ethical stance that emphasizes the value and agency of human beings, individually and collectively.
10. Ulrich and Ulrich (2010).
11. Pink (2009).
12. Pink (2009).
13. Pink (2009).

Chapter 18

1. Greenhouse 5 questions to ask yourself when building an employee alumni program www.greenhouse.io/guidance/5-questions-to-ask-yourself-when-building-an-employee-alumni-program
2. Hoffman, Casnocha, and Yeh (2013).
3. Hoffman, Casnocha, and Yeh (2013).
4. Enterprise Alumni What Are Corporate Alumni Networks? Retrieved from https://enterprisealumni.com/alumni-dictionary/what-are-corporate-alumni-networks/
5. Businesswire (2015).
6. Tucker (2018).
7. Tucker (2018).
8. Tucker (2018).
9. Tucker (2018).
10. Tucker (2018).
11. Enterprise Alumni What Are Corporate Alumni Networks? Retrieved from https://enterprisealumni.com/alumni-dictionary/what-are-corporate-alumni-networks/
12. Hoffman, Casnocha, and Yeh (2013).
13. Schawbel (2012).
14. Hoffman, Casnocha, and Yeh (2013).
15. Webb (2017).
16. Enterprise Alumni What Are Corporate Alumni Networks? Retrieved from https://enterprisealumni.com/alumni-dictionary/what-are-corporate-alumni-networks/
17. Webb (2017).

Action Plan

1. You can contact me at tim@winnersatwork.com.au for further information about the 360-degree assessment.
2. Dr. Tim Baker can be contacted at tim@winnersatwork.com.au

References

"Why Power Skills Are What You Need to Succeed." *UBIS*. Available at https://ubis-geneva.ch/blog/why-power-skills-are-what-you-need-to-succeed/

Ackerman, C.A. 2020. "What is Positive Psychology and Why Is It Important?" PositivePsychology.com

Acton, A. 2017. "How to Stop Wasting 2.5 Hours on Email Every Day." Available from www.forbes.com/sites/annabelacton/2017/07/13/innovators-challenge-how-to-stop-wasting-time-on-emails/?sh=42854cb39788

Autor, D.H. 2015. "Why are There Still So Many Jobs? The History and Future of Workplace Automation." *Journal of Economic Perspectives* 29, no. 3.

Baker, T.B. 2009. *The 8 Values of Highly Productive Companies: Creating Wealth Froma New Employment Relationship.* Brisbane: Australian Academic Press.

Baker, T.B. 2013. *The End of the Performance Review: A New Approach to Appraising Employee Performance.* London: Palgrave Macmillan.

Baker, T.B. 2014. "What is Job Lag?" *Training Journal.* Available at www.trainingjournal.com/blog/what-job-lag

Baker, T.B. 2014. *Attracting and Retaining Talent: Becoming an Employer of Choice.* London: Palgrave Macmillan.

Baker, T.B. 2016. *The End of the Job Description: Shifting From a Job-Focus to a Performance-Focus.* London: Palgrave Macmillan.

Baker, T.B. 2018. *Bringing the Human Being Back to Work: The 10 Performance and Development Conversations Leaders Must Have.* London: Palgrave Macmillan.

Baker, T.B. 2021. *Breaking the Proactive Paradox: Maximizing Performance Through Empowerment.* New York, NY: Business Expert Press.

Berg, J.M., J.E. Dutton, and A.Wrzesniewski. 2007. "What is Job Crafting and Why Does It Matter?" Available from https://positiveorgs.bus.umich.edu/wp-content/uploads/What-is-Job-Crafting-and-Why-Does-it-Matter1.pdf

Bradley, A.J.,and M.P. McDonald. December 2011. "People are not your greatest asset." *Harvard Business Review.*

Brandon Hall Group.2019. "The ROI of Modern Performance Management." Available at: REFLEKTIVE_RESEARCH-BRIEF_FINAL_111219-1.pdf

Brown, S.P., W.L. Cron, and T.W. Leigh. 1993. "Do Feelings of Success Mediate Sales Performance-Work Attitude Relationships?" *Journal of the Academy of Marketing Science* 21, pp. 91–99.

Businesswire.2015. "They're Back! New Survey Reveals Changing Mindset About Boomerang Employees and the Organizations They Once Left." Available from www.businesswire.com/news/home/20150901005843/en/

They%E2%80%99re-Back%21-New-Survey-Reveals-Changing-Mindset-About-Boomerang-Employees-and-the-Organizations-They-Once-Left

Cable, D.M., F. Gino, and R.Staats. 2013. "Reinventing Employee Onboarding."*MIT Sloan Management Review* 54, no. 3.

Caldwell, D.F., and C.A. O'Reilly. 1990. "Measuring Person-Job Fit with a Profile-Comparison Process."*Journal of Applied Psychology* 75, pp. 648–657.

Canady, S. 2021. "Tackling the Transition from Tech Expert to Manager." Available from www.linkedin.com/pulse/tackling-transition-from-tech-expert-manager-sara-canaday/

Carucci, R.A. 2020. "How to Actually Encourage Employee Accountability." *Harvard Business Review.*

Carucci, R.A. 2021. *To Be Honest:Lead with the Power of Truth, Justice and Purpose.* London: Kogan Page.

CEO Magazine.2019. *28 Unforgettable History-Defining Moments of the Past Decade.* Available from: www.theceomagazine.com/business/world-news/historical-moments-decade/

CIPD.2020. *Valuing your talent.* Available from: www.cipd.co.uk/Images/case-study-unilever-260516_tcm18-19991.pdf

Darden, W.R., R. Hampton, and R.D. Howell. 1989. "Career Versus Organizational Commitment: Antecedents and Consequences of Retail Salespeople's Commitment."*Journal of Retailing* 65, pp. 80–105.

Deloitte Global Human Capital Trends.2020. *Superteams: Putting AI in the Group.*

Deloitte Insights.2021. *The Social Enterprise in a World Disrupted: Leading the Shift From, Survive to Thrive 2021 Deloitte Global Human Capital Trends.*

Deutsch, S. 2021. "How can Organisations Adapt to the Rise of Part-Time Work?"*HRM.* Available at www.hrmonline.com.au/topics/hr-strategy-planning-and-measurement/rise-in-part-time-work/

Dr. Tim Baker can be contacted at tim@winnersatwork.com.au

Dubbelt, L., E. Demerouti, and S. Rispens. 2019. "The Value of job Crafting for Work Engagement, Task Performance, and Career Satisfaction: Longitudinal and Quasi-Experimental Evidence." *European Journal of Work and Organizational Psychology* 28, no. 3, pp. 300–314.

Dutton, J.E., and A.Wrzesniewski. 2020. "What Job Crafting Looks Like." *Harvard Business Review.*

Enterprise Alumni What Are Corporate Alumni Networks? Available from https://enterprisealumni.com/alumni-dictionary/what-are-corporate-alumni-networks/

Fernandez, C., G. Nagel, and C. Green. May–June 2021. "The High Cost of Board Succession Planning: A Better Way to Find Your Next CEO." *Harvard Business Review.*

Fernández-Aráoz, C. June 2014. "21st-Century Talent Spotting."*Harvard Business Review.*

Fountaine, T., B. McCarthy, and T. Saleh. July–August 2019. "Building the AI-powered organization." *Harvard Business Review.*

Gallacher, J. 2020. "Remote Work Case Study: LondonEnergy." *HR magazine.* Available at www.hrmagazine.co.uk/content/features/remote-work-case-study-londonenergy

Global Workplace Analytics. 2019. *State of Remote Working 20-19.* Available at 2019 State of Remote Work Report (owllabs.com)

Graeber, D. 2018. *Bullshit Jobs: A Theory.* NY: Simon & Schuster.

Greenhouse 5 questions to ask yourself when building an employee alumni programwww.greenhouse.io/guidance/5-questions-to-ask-yourself-when-building-an-employee-alumni-program

Halbesleben, J.R.B. 2010. "A Meta-Analysis of Work Engagement: Relationships with Burnout, Demands, Resources, and Consequences." In *Work Engagement: A Handbook of Essential Theory and Research*, eds. A.B. Bakker and M.P. Leiter, 102–117. New York, NY: Psychology Press.

Hoffman, R., B. Casnocha, and C. Yeh. 2013. "Tours of Duty: The New Employer-Employee Compact."*Harvard Business Review.*

How Too. Top 3 HR trends in 2021.

Hubstaff blog. 2020. "Are Remote Workers More Productive? We've Checked All the Research So You Don't Have to." Available at https://blog.hubstaff.com/remote-workers-more-productive/

Human Capital Institute.2019. www.hci.org/blog/why-new-employees-quit

Humanism is a philosophical and ethical stance that emphasizes the value and agency of human beings, individually and collectively.

Investors in People. Available from www.investorsinpeople.com/knowledge/onboarding-induction/

Johnson, W. 2019. "What to Do When a Good Employee Stops Trying to Grow." *Harvard Business Review.*

Joseph, D., W.K. Lim, and C.T. Chun. 2018. *Evie.ai: The Rise of Artificial Intelligence and the Future of Work.* Singapore: Nanyang Business School.

Judge, T.A., J.E. Bono, C.J. Thoresen, and G.K. Patton. 2001. "The Job Satisfaction-Job Performance Relationship: A Qualitative and Quantitative Review."*Psychological Bulletin* 127, no.3, pp. 376–407.

Keaveney, S.M., and J.E. Nelson. 1993. "Coping with Organizational Role Stress: Intrinsic Motivational Orientation, Perceived Role Benefits, and Psychological Withdrawal." *Journal of the Academy of Marketing Science* 21, pp. 113–124.

Kouzes, J.M., and B.Z. Posner. 2011. *Credibility: How Leaders Gain and Lose It.* San Francisco: Jossey Bass.

Künn, S., C. Seel,and D.Zegners. 2020."Cognitive Performance in the Home Office—What Professional Chess Can Tell Us." *World of Labor*. Available at https://wol.iza.org/opinions/cognitive-performance-in-the-home-office?utm_source=Adestra&utm_medium=email&utm_content=Cognitive%20performance%20in%20the%20home%20office%E2%80%94What%20professional%20chess%20can%20tell%20us&utm_campaign=IZA%20WoL%20Sept%20monthly%20newsletter

Lombardi, M. 2011. "Onboarding 2011: The Path to Productivity." *Aberdeen Group*. Available from www.talentwise.com/files/Onboarding_2011_-_The_Path_to_Productivity.pdf

MacKenzie, S.B., P.M. Podsakoff, and M.Ahearne. 1998. "Some Possible Antecedents of In-Role and Extra-Role Salesperson Performance."*Journal of Marketing* 62, pp. 87–98.

Mercer.2019. "Transforming HR: Why a Target Interaction Model (TIM) is the Key to Unlocking the Employee Experience." Available from www.mercer.com/our-thinking/career/transforming-hr-why-a-target-interaction-model-is-the-key-to-unlocking-the-employee-experience.html

Middlemiss, N. 2015. "Encouraging the Elusive Work-Life Balance – Are We All Talk?" www.hcamag.com/hr-news/encouraging-the-elusive-worklife-balance--are-we-all-talk-196257.aspx

Miller, G.E. 2021. "70% of Americans Want to be Self-Employed. What is Stopping You?" Available at https://20somethingfinance.com/self-employment-poll/

Morgan, J. 2017. *The Employee Experience Advantage: How to Win the War for Talent by Giving Employees the Workspaces They Want, the Tools They Need, and a Culture They Can Celebrate*. New Jersey, NJ: Wiley.

Murphy, J. 2021. "How to Retain Employees: 20 Practical Takeaways From 8 Case Studies." Available at https://snacknation.com/blog/how-to-retain-employees/

N.A. 2006. "Research and Results: A Look at Current Trends and Data." *Strategic HR Review* 5,no. 3, pp. 14–15. https://doi.org/10.1108/14754390680000875

N.A. 2019. "HBR's 10 Must Reads Series (2019)." *On Reinventing HR*. Boston: Harvard Business Review Press.

O'Hara, C. April 2017. "How to Work with Someone Who isn't a Team Player."*Harvard Business Review*.

On re-inventing HR page 122

Peakon. 2021. The Employee Expectation Report. With over 150 million employee survey responses, and 30 million employee comments, this report offers a comprehensive understanding of how employee expectations have evolved throughout 2020.

Petrou, P., E. Demerouti, M.C.W. Peeters, W.B. Schaufeli, and J.Hetland. 2012. "Crafting a Job on a Daily Basis: Contextual Correlates and the Link to Work Engagement."*Journal of Organizational Behavior 33*, pp. 1120–1141.

Pink, D.H. 2009. *Drive: The Surprising Truth About What Motivates Us*. New York, NY: Riverhead Books.

Pink, D.H. 2010. *Drive: The Surprising Truth About What Motivates Us*. Canongate Books.

Rath, T. 2007. "Strengths Finder 2.0." *Gallup Press*.

Ready, D.A., J.A. Conger, and L.A. Hill. June 2010. "Are You a High Potential?" Harvard Business Review.

Reilly, S. 2017. *The Facilitative Leader: Managing Performance Without Controlling People*. New York, NY: Business Expert Press.

Rokeach, M. 1973. *The Nature of Human Values*. New York, NY: The Free Press.

Root, A. 2021. "Remote Working—Case Studies." Available at www.linkedin.com/pulse/working-remote-case-studies-amanda-root/

Schawbel, D. 2012. "How Companies Can Benefit from Inclusion." *Forbes*.

Schneider, M. 2018. "Costs of Poor Communication Reach $37 Billion." Available from www.inc.com/michael-schneider/the-extrovert-vs-introvert-dynamic-could-be-costing-your-organization-millions-heres-how-to-bridge-communication-gap.html

Senge, P.M. 2006. *The Fifth Discipline: The Art and Practice of the Learning Organization*. London: Random House.

Shore, L.M., and H.J. Martin. 1989. "Job Satisfaction and Organizational Commitment in Relation to Work Performance and Turnover Intentions." *Human Relations* 42, pp. 625–638.

Sneader, K., and B. Sternfels. 2020. "From Surviving to Thriving: Reimagining the Post-COVID-19 Return McKinsey & Company." Available from www.mckinsey.com/featured-insights/future-of-work/from-surviving-to-thriving-reimagining-the-post-covid-19-return

Stapleton, D.F. 2021. "What would a World Without Work Actually Look Like?" Available at www.hrmonline.com.au/future-of-work/a-world-without-work-daniel-susskind/?utm_source=Informz&utm_medium=email&utm_campaign=EDM

Starner, T. 2015. "Study: Workplace Accountability Requires a Specific Strategy." *HR Dive*. Available at Study: Workplace accountability requires a specific strategy | HR Dive

Susskind, D. 2020. *A World Without Work: Technology, Automation, and How We Should Respond*. London: Allen Lane.

Taylor, F.W. 2006. *The Principles of Scientific Management*. NY: Cosimo Classics.

Tiny Pulse.2017. *The Broken Bridges of the Workplace 2017 Employee Engagement Report*. Available at TINYpulse-2017-Employee-Engagement-Report-Broken-Bridges-of-the-Workplace.pdf

Tucker, G. 2018. "Why Companies Should Stay Connected with Ex-Employees." *SHRM*. www.shrm.org/hr-today/news/hr-magazine/0418/pages/corporate-alumni-programs-mean-never-having-to-say-goodbye.aspx

Ulrich, D., and W. Ulrich. 2010. *The Why of Work: How Great Leaders Build Abundant Organizations That Win.* New York, NY: McGraw-Hill.

Valcour, M. 2021. "Transform Your Technical Expertise Into Leadership." *Harvard Business Review.*

Volini, E. et al. April 2019. "From Jobs to Superjobs." *Deloitte insights.*

Warner, J. 2012. *Top 10 Most Valued Job Skills.* http://blog.readytomanage.com/top-10-most-valued-job-skills/

Webb, M. 2017. "5 Ways to Build an Alumni Network and A Recruiting Machine." *Forbes.*

Weber, L. 2016. "CEOs No Longer Say 'People Are Our Greatest Asset,' According to New Report." *Wall Street Journal.* Available at www.wsj.com/articles/ceos-no-longer-say-people-are-our-greatest-asset-according-to-new-report-1479412130

Welsh, J. 2019. "5 Case Studies in Successful Succession Planning." *Forbes.* Available from www.forbes.com/sites/johnwelsheurope/2019/01/17/5-case-studies-in-successful-succession-planning/?sh=130023423728

Work Institute. 2019. "Retention Report." Available athttps://info.workinstitute.com/hubfs/2019%20Retention%20Report/Work%20Institute%202019%20Retention%20Report%20final-1.pdf

Wrzesniewski, A., J.M. Berg, and J.E. Dutton. 2010. "Managing Yourself: Turn the Job You Have into the Job You Want." *Harvard Business Review* 88, no. 6, pp. 114–117.

www.akyra.com.au/induction-onboarding

www.amazon.com/World-Without-Email-Reimagining-Communication-ebook/dp/B08BKSJX1M

www.bqint.com/index.php/onboarding-isnt-enough/

www.britannica.com/technology/Model-T

www.forbes.com/sites/tracybrower/2021/01/17/think-productivity-with-work-from-home-is-improving-think-again-heres-what-you-must-know/?sh=51bb8aaa2d67

www.talentlms.com/blog/remote-work-statistics-survey/

www.thomas.co/assessments/workplace-personality-tests

Yeung, R. 2011. *I is for Influence: The new science of persuasion.* London: Macmillan.

You can contact me at tim@winnersatwork.com.au for further information about the 360-degree assessment.

About the Author

Dr. Tim Baker is a thought leader, international consultant, and successful author. Tim is managing director of WINNERS-at-WORK Pty Ltd, which specializes in leadership development and performance (www.winnersatwork.com.au).

He was recently voted one of *The Most Talented Global Training & Development Leaders* by the World HRD Congress, which is awarded by a distinguished international panel of professionals "who are doing extraordinary work" in the field of HRD. In 2018, Tim was a Finalist in the *Learning Professional of the Year* for the Asia Pacific Institute of Learning Professionals Awards. His consulting firm WINNERS-at-WORK Pty Ltd was listed in the *Top 10 Change Management Consulting Service Companies* in APAC 2020 (HR Tech Outlook).

Tim completed his Doctoral degree in 2005 at QUT. He has served on QUT Council for over 11-years.

Tim has conducted over 2,430 seminars, workshops, and keynote addresses to over 45,000 people in 12 countries across 21 industry groups and regularly writes for HR industry press. Tim can be contacted at tim@winnersatwork.com.au.

Tim lives in Brisbane, Australia with his wife Carol. He has two daughters.

Connect with Tim online

Contact me at tim@winninersatwork.com.au
LinkedIn: www.linkedin.com/in/winnersatwork/
Facebook: www.facebook.com/winnersatworkptyltd
Twitter: https://twitter.com/winnersatwork
Instagram: www.instagram.com/winnersatwork/
Pinterest: www.pinterest.com.au/winnersatwork/
YouTube: www.youtube.com/c/TimBakerthoughtleader
SlideShare: www.slideshare.net/DrTimBaker

Index

OTHER TITLES IN THE HUMAN RESOURCE MANAGEMENT AND ORGANIZATIONAL BEHAVIOR COLLECTION

Michael Provitera, Barry University, Editor

- *Versatility in the Age of Specialization* by Angela Cotellessa
- *Embracing Ambiguity* by Michael Edmondson
- *Breaking the Proactive Paradox* by Tim Baker
- *The Modern Trusted Advisor* by MacKay Nancy and Weiss Alan
- *Achieving Success as a 21st Century Manager* by Dean E. Frost
- *A.I. and Remote Working* by Miller Tony
- *Best Boss!* by Ferguson Duncan, Toni M. Pristo, and John Furcon
- *Managing for Accountability* by Curry Lynne
- *Fundamentals of Level Three Leadership* by Clawson James G.S.
- *Emotional Connection: The EmC Strategy* by Gershfeld Lola and Sedehi Ramin
- *Civility at Work* by Bayer Lewena
- *Lean on Civility* by Masotti Christian and Bayer Lewena
- *Agility* by Edmondson Michael
- *Strengths Oriented Leadership* by Beadle Matt

Concise and Applied Business Books

The Collection listed above is one of 30 business subject collections that Business Expert Press has grown to make BEP a premiere publisher of print and digital books. Our concise and applied books are for...

- Professionals and Practitioners
- Faculty who adopt our books for courses
- Librarians who know that BEP's Digital Libraries are a unique way to offer students ebooks to download, not restricted with any digital rights management
- Executive Training Course Leaders
- Business Seminar Organizers

Business Expert Press books are for anyone who needs to dig deeper on business ideas, goals, and solutions to everyday problems. Whether one print book, one ebook, or buying a digital library of 110 ebooks, we remain the affordable and smart way to be business smart. For more information, please visit www.businessexpertpress.com, or contact sales@businessexpertpress.com.

www.ingramcontent.com/pod-product-compliance
Lightning Source LLC
Chambersburg PA
CBHW061200220326
41599CB00025B/4550